MW00625661

God's Heart through a Horse's Eyes

By

Bethany Tuskey

DEDICATION

To my loving wife, Nicole, thank you for walking
with me on this journey of life, and for your
continuous support and encouragement.

To our son, Ezekiel, may you know that you are
loved deeply by your parents and by your Creator.
Chase your dreams and live a life of adventure.

To my horse, Ilustre, who started me on an
incredible journey with God, as well as to all of the
horses who have passed through my life and given
of themselves to teach me more about love, grace,
and the heart of God.

CONTENTS

INTRODUCTION

"If I can put one touch of a rosy sunset into the life of any man or woman, I shall feel that I have worked with God." *Henry David Thoreau*

At Tuskey Dressage, my horse training and performance company, we believe that God has entrusted us and equipped us to take care of His creations. Our spirituality plays a vital role in our horse training. We strive daily to live in a way that is pleasing to our Holy Father including training horses in a way that He would approve. We constantly seek God's guidance in the care and training of our horses and in the daily operations of our business. We believe it is through God's grace that we have been so successful. He has truly blessed us. We hope to share these blessings with others. God has touched our lives; we wouldn't be where we are without Him.

We handle and train our horses in a way that fosters a strong bond with them. This cannot be done through force, harsh bits, spurs or other gadgets. It must be done through kindness and love. By developing a spiritual connection with a horse, you can achieve a relationship that transcends anything you ever dreamed possible. You will have a horse that truly desires to be with you, wants to come to you and dance with you. Both you and your horse will be able to freely express yourselves. You, too, can have a relationship reminiscent of the riders in the movie <u>Avatar</u>, in *which you need only think what you want, and your horse will respond with gladness.*

After all, isn't that what you've always wanted?

While God can always show us a better way of connecting with our horses, the horses can also show us the path to a better relationship with God. For example, equids appear many times in the Bible from Balaam's donkey, the only animal in the Bible to ever talk, to Mary riding a donkey to Bethlehem and Jesus riding a donkey into Jerusalem, and even Jesus returning triumphantly to Earth at the end of times on a majestic white horse.

We have been blessed by God with four incredible horses that have come into our lives in extraordinary ways. Ilustre, our Andalusian gelding, two Andalusian mares- Anna and Maia, and our most recent addition- Anna's first filly, Ariel. All four have taught us something unique and special about life and love and all four have brought us closer to God in ways we never would have imagined.

The lessons I, personally, have learned have brought me on an incredible journey in knowing God and knowing myself. I hope that through these stories, you too will be able to start a journey of your own that will bring you closer to our Father in Heaven. Whether you have owned horses all your life, or simply have always loved them, it is my prayer that you would take to heart the lessons that they have for us.

One thing I know for certain- God is so good and I am only just beginning to realize how incredible that is.

Horses and humans have been working together for thousands of years. Horses are spiritual creatures and can help us to become more spiritual. They live the way that God designed them to, true to themselves and to those around them, and to their Creator. By observing them, and working with them, they can show us a better way to live, bringing us closer to our Creator. Horses have taught me, and all of us at Tuskey Dressage, many lessons which I share with you now in the hopes that it will inspire and encourage you.

Joy, Peace, Patience, Forgiveness, and Unconditional Love will fill your life as you learn to walk the path that God has laid out for you.

And the horse will guide you on your journey.

CHAPTER ONE:
ILUSTRE'S STORY

"All of our dreams can come true if we have the courage to pursue them" Walt Disney

Everybody serves and worships God in different ways. For some it is music, others it is teaching, and for others, leading. For me, it is through working with and caring for His amazing creations, specifically horses. God made these creatures for us to enjoy, but also for us to see His awesome power and to worship Him by enjoying and caring for them. Everything in creation was made by God and belongs to Him; we are only stewards. St. Francis of Assisi believed it was the "duty of men to protect and enjoy nature as both the stewards of God's creation and as creatures ourselves." This means treating the animals God has given us with respect and loving them as God has loved us.

God's creations can also teach us about God and how to live our lives the way God wants. Through God's creatures, we can come to a better relationship with God himself. If we let them, horses can reveal to us areas of our lives where we need to change or improve. Dominique Barbier, a master trainer, states that "The horse is the mirror of your soul, of who you really are. It is your reflection that you see through his eyes."[1] If you give the horse love, he will give it back. If you give him a sense of fun and adventure, he will give that back. Likewise, if you approach a horse with fear, anger, anxiety or impatience, that is what you will receive back from the horse.

Everything that separates us from God, separates us from having the perfect relationship with our horse-anger, pride, fear, impatience, self-centeredness. This is why horses interact more readily with children; they sense the child's innocence and joy. For this same reason, Jesus commands us to be like little children, to let go of everything holding us back and to freely give of ourselves to Him. Horses can guide us on this path and by learning how to better interact with them, we can learn how to better interact with both God and our fellow humans. Horses give us a glimpse of the love the Father has for us and if we treat them right, horses will freely share that love with us.

———————————

I started working with horses at a young age. One of my greatest passions is sharing the magic of horses with people who don't get to experience it every day. I do this by performing at horse fairs, parades, and renaissance festivals. Our troupe of riders and horses get decked out in costumes and ride to music showcasing the beauty and power of these magnificent creatures. I have always imagined what it would be like to live in a magical land such as Narnia or Middle Earth. Through these performances, I get to live out those dreams.

Working with horses has taught me some important life lessons. Horses are wonderful teachers if we are willing to listen to what they have to say. Many horses have come and gone through my life and each has had something to teach me, from the wizened old school horse that takes extra care, giving confidence to the nervous beginner but also keeps the cocky older student humble by spooking unexpectedly, to the difficult young stallion that teaches an eager young trainer patience, not to take things personally, and that it's ok to make mistakes and not be so perfect. They all inspired me to chase after my dreams and to achieve greatness.

I was raised in a church but never developed a personal relationship with God. I never really understood just how deep God's love was for me or how powerful His grace. Church, to me, was nothing more than a weekly obligation and so, as I got older, I stopped attending. I figured I was doing well since, for the most part, I was a good person. But God wanted more from me and more for me. So, He began drawing me nearer.

God is infinitely powerful and capable of using things in our lives to draw us closer to Him, teaching us about how He wants us to live. This has been true for me. Horses have been such a large part of my life that it was natural for God to use a horse to bring me back to Him.

My horse, Ilustre, truly was a gift from God. He came into my life in such a magical way. Loving horses doesn't always mean being able to afford one. I've worked long hours to earn precious moments in the saddle. As a child and a teenager, I could never afford to have a horse of my own, so I took lessons, volunteered at a stable, and eventually did an internship with a trainer. I felt such a strong longing to simply be around these magnificent animals.

I will always remember that day when I first saw a picture of the horse that would change my life. The photo showed a beautiful white Andalusian gelding. An Andalusian- the horse of kings! My very own Shadowfax! His owner was not looking to sell him. She simply wanted to find him a good home where he would be loved and cared for. I could never have bought such an incredible horse, and yet things like money don't matter to God. He had a plan for me and for Ilustre. The very next day, Ilustre stepped off the trailer, into his new stall, and the journey began.

Ilustre's name is a term used in Spanish to mean "wise or all-knowing one". How true that was...I didn't yet realize how much he had to teach me, not just about riding, but about life, and more importantly, about God.

Unfortunately, this magnificent animal had been damaged by some of his previous experiences. Ilustre was explosive during riding, rearing and bolting without warning. It took a lot of patience and love to teach him that it was acceptable to trust again. I struggled with this for a long time. There were moments where I would see a glimmer of the potential in this horse, but these moments were brief. For the most part he remained aloof and distrusting. He was emotionally shut down despite my efforts. I couldn't get through to him.

This was incredibly difficult for me. I have always struggled with self-doubt and fear of failure. However, I had learned to overcome these things by working hard so I would achieve my goals. I took comfort in the work. Each time I accomplished a new goal, I would temporarily feel better about myself. I would keep myself busy to avoid facing my feelings of failure. This was true in my daily life. See, over the years I had learned to be self-sufficient and if I encountered a problem along the way, I would just dig in and work hard and get through it. So, that's what I did with Ilustre. I tried everything I could think of. I read books. I took lessons. I tried different training methods. Nothing worked. In fact, the harder I tried, the worse things became.

I was now flooded with self-doubt. How could I ever be a great horse trainer if I couldn't even train my own horse? I felt like a failure. My feelings overwhelmed me to the point where I no longer enjoyed riding; fear and anger ruled my life. Others around me had no idea that anything was wrong. I was very good at putting on a mask and pretending everything was fine, but I truly struggled to get through each day. I was surviving, but that was about it. I was unhappy nearly all the time. How many of you have been there? Someone asks how you are doing, and you smile and say, "Oh, I'm fine," but deep down you are crying out for help.

Others may not have known anything was wrong, but Ilustre sure did. Horses are far more in tune with energy and emotions than people ever will be, therefore Ilustre was well aware that I was not happy. He felt my fear and anger, reflecting it right back at me. We were both on a downward spiral and I was ready to quit. I almost did. Instead, I prayed.

And God answered.

It was through my struggles with Ilustre, and my desire to give up, that I first realized I needed to seek God's help. That this situation wasn't something I could do on my own through my own abilities. This concept was new to me since I had grown to be self-reliant and self- sufficient. I was now desperate. So, I started praying and I began reading the Bible.

It was then that God showed me the verse Exodus 14:14 "The Lord will fight for you; you need only to be still."

Wow, really God? Do nothing? That can't be the answer. That won't work. I'm a work-a-holic, remember? There's got to be something I can do. I don't think I can be still.... but I guess I'll try. After all, nothing else has worked...

Matthew Henry's commentary on Exodus 14:14 reads, "Stand still, think not to save yourselves either by fighting or flying; wait for God's orders, and observe them. Compose yourselves, by confidence in God, into peaceful thoughts of the great salvation God is about to work for you. If God brings his people into straits, he will find a way to bring them out."[2]

I started going into the barn early in the mornings and working with Ilustre at liberty, free of ropes, bridles or saddle. This helped me connect with him without the distraction of the equipment, and without the pressure to perform. I found that the best way to earn Ilustre's trust was to simply spend time with him, learning to enjoy each other's presence. It was liberating to have no particular goal in mind, but simply to enjoy the presence of my horse and of God. Ilustre was tormented by fear and I was on an unrelenting quest for perfection. Together, we learned what it meant to enjoy life. The transformation in both of us was remarkable! From then on, everything was different.

Sometimes in our busy schedules, in our world that is full of pressure to perform, we forget to slow down and simply enjoy the life God has given us, trusting that He will take care of us. God used Ilustre to teach me this and by improving my relationship with this horse, I was able to improve my relationship with God.

I realized what was missing in my life - spending time in God's presence. God laid it on my heart that I needed to find a church home. Not long after those feelings arose, my wife, Nicole, and I walked into a small church in an industrial building. The first day we went, the church happened to be preparing for their Vacation Bible School and was completely decked out to look like a medieval castle. Coincidence? I think not. God had placed us exactly where we needed to be. It was the beginning of a crazy, unbelievable journey.

Horses live in the moment with no regrets about the past or worries about the future. Horses love unconditionally. Horses forgive and do not hold grudges. Horses do not worry about what other horses think about them. Horses do not judge each other. They live freely as God intended them to. Horses have taught me to see each day as a gift and to appreciate the little things in life. To always be thankful for my blessings and to live my life passionately. I have learned the power of dreaming big, working hard, and praying even harder. I have learned to overcome fear and self-doubt because my Lord loves me no matter what. Most importantly, I have learned to trust in the power of my God for He is an awesome God.

I've learned how to be still; to notice the little things.

When was the last time you really took time to notice the world around you? The birds chirping, the warmth of the sun, a gentle breeze blowing. Nowadays, people lead very hectic lives. Who has time to stop and notice the flower growing by the side of the road?

These little things are so important! We are overlooking the awesomeness of God's creation! We need to slow down for a moment and realize what we are missing. Peace, beauty, grace, power; they are all out there, and we need to see them!

For that matter, who has time for God? To really spend time with Him, praying, worshiping, noticing His incredible creations? God always has time for us, yet it is so easy to forget about Him in our busy lives. We have forgotten how to be in the moment, to be present. We are so busy and driven to succeed as if we must always be doing something.

I have a young horse that I am working with right now who has exactly this problem. She must always be in motion- chewing on something, moving her head around, pawing the ground. She is unable to simply stand still. Each day I spend a little time with her just doing nothing. At first, she tries everything she can think to be in motion, but eventually she stops and, for a few moments, is at peace. Each day, these moments last a little bit longer.

Sometimes in life we are like the young horse. We are unhappy with our lives, so we try different things to make ourselves happy. We may find a new job, begin a new diet, work harder and do more. All we really need to do is stop trying so hard and just allow things to happen. It is in God's plan for us.

I encourage equestrians to spend time with their horses with the purpose being simply to enjoy being with each other. This time can be spent while they are eating, while working with them at liberty, or even while riding. Take a few moments to stop and reflect. This is how positive relationships are developed. Many people have a strict routine when they come to the barn- groom, saddle, ride, unsaddle, and leave. Even worse, some people have their horses already saddled for them so all they have to do is show up and ride. If this is all you ever do with your horse, you are missing out on something very special.

It takes time to develop a relationship with a horse. Horses will very often develop strong relationships with each other. They eat together, rest together, play together, and just stand around doing nothing together. This is vitally important to the bonding process. If we want to develop a relationship with our horses, we need to be willing to put the same amount of time and commitment. Bonds aren't built from the saddle. They are built on the ground. Spend time with your horse while he is eating or resting. Spend time standing around doing nothing with him.

In order to be a good rider, one must learn the value of developing a relationship with the horse. Horses aren't machines, and when they are treated as such, the rider will only ever achieve mechanical, forced results. Horses, just like people, have individual personalities. By spending time with the horse, one can learn what they like and don't like and how to best work with them, training them to achieve the greatest results based on their unique personality.

Horses don't care about the ribbons. They don't care about the fancy equipment or the fancy clothes like the riders in the magazines. They don't care about the expensive supplements or cool toys. They care about the time spent with them. Time spent doing simple things like grooming, feeding, groundwork and just being around them.

When two horses like each other, they spend all their time together. They eat together, groom each other and stand around doing nothing together. They do it because they simply enjoy being in each other's presence.

Be still. Spend time with the horse beyond riding. Just stand in the stall and breathe.

Be still. Spend time with God. Bask in the glory of His presence and breathe.

Developing a relationship with God is like that of a horse. You can't have a good relationship if you don't put the time in. That means enjoying some quiet time where it is just you and Him, soaking up the love He pours out on you.

Every day, I get to experience God's glory in a very real way. Nature has a profound way of showing off God's power. I see sunsets that take your breath away, snow sparkling in the morning sun, fog settling in the pastures so I can just make out the silhouettes of my horses, and thousands of stars lighting up the night sky. I've seen new life and the end of life.

Since this magical horse, Ilustre, came into my life and took me on a journey that led me to know God, everything has changed. I no longer struggle to get through each day. I have learned to be content with myself and where I am at in life. It hasn't always been easy, and I still have a hard time with some things but now I take confidence in knowing that God loves me and is always with me. The struggles are only temporary. I have learned to see and appreciate all of the blessings that I have been given. I have found a peace and joy that I could never have dreamed possible.

And it all started with a horse.

CHAPTER TWO:
OVERCOMING FEAR

"Do you give the horse his strength or clothe his neck with a flowing mane? Do you make him leap like a locust, striking terror with his proud snorting? It paws fiercely, rejoicing in its strength, and charges into the fray. It laughs at fear, afraid of nothing; it does not shy away from the sword. The quiver rattles against its side, along with the flashing spear and lance. In frenzied excitement it eats up the ground; it cannot stand still when the trumpet sounds." Job 39: 19-24

This passage in Job describes the warhorse as strong, fierce, fearless and excited. What's interesting is the way the horse is described- not as a timid, fearful creature but as a strong, powerful force. When left to their own devices, most horses will be naturally timid. As a prey animal, this is what has allowed them to survive for so many thousands of years. However, under the loving guidance of a good leader, a horse can become fearless and strong.

Horses overcome their greatest fears to be with us. It is not natural for a predator and prey to be able to come together the way a human and a horse can. Many people take for granted the fact the horses can be ridden. But in fact, it is really quite amazing. When a mountain lion wants to kill a horse, it jumps on the horse's back and wraps its claws around the horse's body. Because of this, horses have a strong survival instinct to not allow anything on their backs. Then, along comes a human, who looks and smells like a predator. This human takes a saddle, which, by the way, is made out of the skins of another dead animal, and places it on the horse's back. The human then climbs onto the saddle and wraps his legs around the horse. And the horse allows it. He even allows the rider to direct his movements. It is a horse's natural instinct to be afraid but when he trusts his rider, he is able to overcome that fear and become obedient to the rider.

We need to trust in our Lord, and he will help us overcome our fears and be obedient to him.

Like the horse, humans are naturally fearful creatures. Fear can severely limit what we are capable of doing with our lives. After all, as the saying goes "doubt kills more dreams than failure ever will." However, when we accept Jesus as our Lord and Savior, and put our trust in Him, He fills us with His Holy Spirit and give us strength. His Spirit guides us and directs us and is faithful to us, so we learn to trust Him. This gives us courage and strength to overcome our fears.

God describes us in this way in 2 Timothy 1:7 which reads "For God has not given us a spirit of fear, but of power, and of love, and of a sound mind." (KJV)

The attitude of the warhorse is the mind of every disciple of Christ, ready and armed to battle and live for the will of God.

Our strength comes from the Lord. Isaiah 41:10 reads "So do not fear, for I am with you do not be dismayed, for I am your God. I will strengthen you and help you; I will uphold you with my righteous right hand."

Deuteronomy 31:6 tells us "Be strong and courageous. Do not be afraid or terrified because of them, for the Lord your God goes with you; he will never leave you nor forsake you."

David proclaims in Psalm 27:1 "The Lord is my light and my salvation; whom shall I fear? The Lord is the stronghold of my life- of whom shall I be afraid?"

Under the guidance of a good rider, the horse is transformed from a fearful, timid creature into a powerful, unstoppable force. The rider is able to bring out the inner strength, beauty, and the majesty of the horse. Under the guidance of God, we are transformed from fearful and uncertain into confident and unstoppable. God brings out the best in us just as the rider does for the horse.

In Psalm 18:29 David writes "In your strength I can crush an army; with my God I can scale any wall." (NLT). David was like the warhorse, and so shall we be. God has called us to a battle, a spiritual battle against the enemy. The stakes are high. We are fighting for the lost souls. We are fighting for our own souls. We can take confidence in knowing that we do not fight alone. God is with us. The Creator of the heavens and earth is fighting with us. The God who heals the sick, raises the dead, quiets the roaring lion, stops the thunderous storms, walks on water, and has conquered death is always with us. He will never leave us. He will never forsake us. He gives us strength to fight.

Fear can be tricky to deal with. Worry can control our lives, preventing us from moving forward, and taking away our joy.

Horses deal with fear in a logical step by step process.
1.   Something triggers the horse to feel fear (or pain, discomfort, frustration, etc.)
2.   The horse acknowledges the emotion

and does something to change it. This is where the flight or fight instinct kicks in. The horse may decide to run, may kick out to defend itself, or he may realize that in this instance he does not need to react.

3. The horse then resumes whatever it was doing prior to the trigger of the emotion

Here's an example to illustrate this process:

A horse is out in a pasture grazing. He is in a relaxed state when a loud noise causes a fear response in him. The horse immediately acknowledges the emotion and reacts to it. He may determine that the noise was not something to fear in which case he will simply go back to grazing. If the horse determines that there is something to be afraid of then the flight or fight response will take over. His first choice when he is afraid is to run away to what he feels is a safe distance. Once he feels he is safe, he will go back to grazing. If flight is not an option, the horse will instead fight until he no longer feels threatened. Once the danger has been dealt with, he goes back to grazing. This whole process usually happens within seconds. It's important to note that when a horse feels fear, he recognizes it, acknowledges it, does something to change it, and then returns to his normal life. He does not waste time trying to figure out where the noise came from or if it's going to happen again or why it happened to him, or how horrible his life is. He simply moves on.

This gives us an example of how we can handle worries that we, as humans, experience.

1. First, acknowledge the emotion you are feeling. Trying to repress it only makes things worse. For example, acknowledge that you are afraid of falling off.
2. Next, determine what action you need to take. If you truly are in danger, then it is best to remove yourself from the situation. This could be getting off, getting someone to help you, or moving to another location.
3. If there is no real danger, then the emotion can be dealt with in a different way. Worry is simply your brain imagining what could possibly go wrong. You can change this emotion by, instead, focusing on everything going right. This could mean focusing on your balanced position in the saddle, the way your horse is focused on you, or maybe some things you've already accomplished during your ride.
4. Once the perceived danger has passed, it is important to move on and not dwell on it. As a natural worrier, I can tell you that this is easier said than done but it is important and can be life changing.

Horses react to anger and frustration in a similar way. They acknowledge the emotion, respond to it, and then move on with their lives. We can take this whole process and apply it to our lives.

When we worry about something, hosting a successful event for example, we need to first acknowledge the fear and determine where it is coming from, and then we can act on it. We can make sure that everything is prepared well ahead of time, that everything is organized and ready to go, and that we haven't overlooked any details. After that, we need to move on. Continuing to stress over the event as it approaches doesn't do any good. We must let go of our fears and focus on the good. It's hard to do, but God is here to help. All we have to do is tell him our fears and then trust in him to take care of things. His promises are true, and his Word can be trusted. God is sovereign and He is working all things together for good and for those who love him (Romans 8:28). If we are living according to God's purposes, we have nothing to worry about.

Visualization is a great tool to help us overcome our worries. Instead of focusing on what could go wrong, we turn our focus toward everything going right.

Visualization is very important when communicating with a horse. Too many people try to do everything physically without even considering the mental side of riding. Horses don't speak to each other with words, so they have to communicate in other ways. This includes visualization. When you want to ask your horse to do something, start by visualizing exactly what you want him to do. You will find that when you use visualization, the amount you have to do physically will decrease. Visualize being successful and your horse responding the way you want him too.

Visualization can be applied to all aspects of life. Your thoughts become your actions and your actions become your destiny. Are you a positive person? Happy? Stressed? Anxious? It all starts with your thoughts. I've mentioned that I am a natural worrier. The best way I've discovered to combat this is to sit in a quiet place and visualize a peaceful situation, such as my horse grazing in a sunny pasture on a warm spring day.

Paul tells us in Philippians 4:8, "Finally, brothers, whatever is true, whatever is honorable, whatever is just, whatever is pure, whatever is lovely, whatever is commendable, if there is any excellence, if there is anything worthy of praise, think about these things."

"These, Paul would say, are the fruit and the food of the mind that is guarded by the peace of God. When we put these good things into our mind, they stay in our mind and then come forth from us" (David Guzik)[3]

We need to keep our thoughts on Jesus. Evil is all around us and if we focus on the evil it will overcome us. But if we put our trust in Jesus, we have nothing to fear for he has already overcome the world, even evil and death itself. We need to focus on Him. When things of the world begin to take over our thoughts, we need to recognize this and then immediately turn back to Jesus by praying, reading the Word, or worshipping. The devil doesn't want us to do these things because he knows they will make us stronger and therefore him weaker. So, he does whatever he can to keep us at arm's length from God. He makes us busy; he gives us things to worry about, things that hurt us, things that distract us. But you need to know that the devil has no power over you unless you choose to relinquish it to him. If you are a Christian, Jesus lives in you, strengthens you, and guides you. The same power that raised Christ from the dead is living inside of you!

"And if the Spirit of him who raised Jesus from the dead is living in you, he who raised Christ from the dead will also give life to your mortal bodies because of his Spirit who lives in you." (Romans 8:11)

I often tell my students to look where they are going while they are riding.

You should look where you are going spiritually as well. Look to Jesus. Go to Jesus.

———————————

So how do we learn to trust Jesus? Good news! He gives us the tools we need. But we need to learn how to use those tools and practice with them in order to be successful.

I'm sure you've heard the saying "Practice makes perfect". Well, I hate to be the bearer of bad news, but this is not necessarily a true statement. Continuously doing something wrong is not going to make you do it right. Now, that's not to say that repetition won't make you better at something (which is where the statement originally came from), but you need to be correct in your repetition or you will not improve.

Imagine two different riders each practicing for an hour a day. One rider has a definite plan for what she is going to achieve, and she works diligently for the entire hour. She is precise in her work, she is continuously checking to make sure both she and her horse are in the proper position, and she works to the best of her ability for the entire hour. The second rider also practices for an hour, but much of that hour is spent standing around talking to her friends or walking lazily around the arena. Her position is sloppy, and her horse is out of balance, but she doesn't bother to correct it. She doesn't have a plan and she doesn't push herself. Both of these two riders have "practiced" for the same amount of time, but they will certainly not achieve the same results. That is why it is important to be correct and diligent in your practice.

A more accurate statement would be "practice makes predictable". In times of stress and trial, you will instinctively fall back on your training. This is when you will truly see how correct your practice had been. This happens all the time with horses.

For example, when you go to a horse show if you have practiced well you will be able to perform well even under the stresses of being in a new place, having others watch you and judge your performance, and being surrounded by other horses, people, and other activities which can be distracting to your horse. However, if you haven't taken the time to practice, or your practice hasn't been very good, then you most likely will not be able to stand up to the stresses of being at a horse show and your performance will suffer.

Another example is a horse that unexpectedly spooks. If you have practiced well and worked hard, your instincts will take over and you will be able to calmly and effectively bring the situation back under control. However, if you haven't taken the time to practice, or your practice hasn't been very good, then when something unexpected happens, you will likely panic and therefore not be able to handle it.

It is the same with your spiritual life. It is easy to trust God and be obedient to him when everything is going well, and things are easy. But this is the time when you need to be practicing and preparing so that when hard times come, which they will, you are ready to deal with them. You must be diligent in your practice or you will never improve.

We are in a spiritual battle. The enemy is constantly attacking us with lies, deceit, and accusations. Ephesians 6:12 states "For our struggle is not against flesh and blood, but against the rulers, against the authorities, against the powers of this dark world and against the spiritual forces of evil in the heavenly realms."

The enemy is constantly trying to draw us away from God. The enemy does not want us to come into full realization of the love God has for us and the power that we have been given through Christ.

But Jesus is stronger than anything that the enemy can throw at us. Ephesians 1:20 tells us that Jesus is "far above all rule and authority, power and dominion, and every name that is invoked, not only in the present age, but also in the one to come."

Paul then goes on to tell us how we are to overcome the fears and struggles in our lives:

"Therefore put on the full armor of God, so that when the day of evil comes, you may be able to stand your ground, and after you have done everything, to stand." (Ephesians 6:13)

If we are going to be warriors, we are going to need some armor. If we are going to be successful, it is important that we understand each piece of the armor. We must know its function and how we can use it to defend ourselves against the attacks of the enemy.

The Belt of Truth, the knowledge and belief in the Truth of God's Word, is essential to our success. We must believe that God is who He says He is and that His promises for us are true. It is important to recognize right from wrong, what God asks us to do and what He forbids us to do, and to recognize that our only hope and salvation is through Him.

The Breastplate of Righteousness is the righteousness that comes from God. We cannot be righteous on our own. We will always fail. However, we are made righteous through Jesus by His death on the cross for our sins. His sacrifice allowed us to receive His righteousness.

The Sandals of The Gospel, or the foundation on which you stand, which gives you firm footing in everything you do. There is a saying "no hoof, no horse". If a horse's hoof becomes damaged it affects everything the horse does. If the damage is bad enough, it can cripple or even lead to death. A horse with weak hooves will always struggle in the work it does. In the same way, we must have a strong foundation of faith based on the Gospel or we will struggle in our work and eventually may even be crippled in our faith.

The Shield of Faith is a shield protecting us from the attacks of the enemy. Satan uses all kinds of attacks against us such as lies, deceptions, accusations, and twisted truths. He uses our feelings and emotions against us to convince us of things that aren't true. Faith allows us to stand against these attacks. We must have faith in God knowing that he does not lie, and his Word is true...yesterday, today, and forever.

The Helmet of Salvation lets us know that it can be easy to get discouraged when going through difficult times, but we are reminded of our salvation which gives us hope. Hope, knowing that because of what Jesus did for us, we have been saved. Hope, knowing that trials are temporary. Hope, knowing that we will spend eternity in Heaven with God.

The Sword of the Spirit, which is the Word of God helps us to defend ourselves against the attacks of the enemy. We must first know the Word in order to be able to use it. It takes practice to become proficient with a sword in order to be able to defend yourself when the time comes. You can't just pick up a sword and expect to be able to go out into battle and defend properly. Likewise, it takes practice to become proficient with the Word. We must spend time reading and studying. The Spirit helps us with this. He provides clarity and understanding to us as we study the Word. This prepares us to be able to defend ourselves.

God gives us the tools we need. It is up to us to choose to use them and we must diligently practice with them. One thing we can be certain of is that He will be with us every step of the way. He will take away our fears and replace them with His strength and courage.

We, too, will be proud and fierce as a war horse.

CHAPTER THREE:
FOLLOWING GOD

"You can never rely on a horse that is educated by fear! There will always be something that he fears more than you. But when he trusts you, he will ask you what to do when he is afraid."
Antoine de Pluvinel

When we ride our horses, we ask them to move where we want, in the direction we want, at the speed we want. To stop, turn, and move when we tell them. This all seems normal to us. However, think about this from the horse's perspective. When we ask him to walk forward, he has no idea where we are going to take him. Will he be safe, or will we lead him into danger? Will the path be easy and smooth, or will it be rough and difficult? How long will he have to keep going? How fast? How far? Will he be able to rest? Will his needs and desires be met? The horse knows none of these things, and yet if he trusts his rider, he will willingly take that first step and then keep going, never knowing what is going to happen next, but simply following the direction of his master.

Oh, if we could only live our lives this way! We may never know exactly what God has planned for us or where He is taking us. Will the path be difficult? How long will it take? When will we be able to rest? Will our needs and desires be met?

God doesn't give us all the details; He just asks us to follow His leading. Unfortunately, instead of trusting Him, many of us try to force things to happen in our own time and our own ways.

Take for example Adam and Eve. Rather than trusting that God had their best interests in mind, they decided to do what they wanted and eat from the tree that God had forbidden. Their actions enabled evil and death to enter the world. Disobedience to God leads to destruction.

Take also Abram and Sarai. Despite his old age, God had promised Abram that he would have a son and be the father of a great nation. Many years had passed and still Sarai was unable to have a child. So, she decided to take matters into her own hands. She allowed Abram to have a child with her servant, Hagar instead. This was not God's plan. Their actions led to much unnecessary difficulty and suffering that could have been avoided had they simply trusted God. Eventually, God did fulfill His promise and Sarai gave birth to a son just as God had said she would.

And then there was Jonah. God called Jonah to preach to the people of Ninevah, but Jonah wanted no part of that plan. He tried to run from God, and he ended up spending three days in the belly of a whale, before eventually repenting and accepting God's purpose for his life, which resulted in many people being saved.

How much difficulty could we avoid if we trusted God more? How many blessings do we miss out on because we are not obedient?

Trusting God is hard. It is not something that comes naturally.

The term "Natural Horsemanship" has become very popular in horse training lately as people seek new and more humane ways of working with their horses. Within this category, there is a broad spectrum of training methods, some of which are quite humane while others are downright abusive. Yet, they all fall under the label of "natural horsemanship". The main problem with this idea of "natural horsemanship" is that there is nothing natural about a human riding a horse.

Horses are prey animals. As such, they have strong

instincts and highly tuned senses to alert them to potential danger. Humans are predators. Humans look like predators, move like predators, and smell like predators. Everything about us tells the horse that we are a predator. It doesn't matter how we change our movements or how we interact with the horse or if we make eye contact or turn our backs to them a certain way. We are still predators and the horse knows that we are still a predator. There's nothing natural about a horse interacting with a predator. Horses can learn that humans will not harm them, but this is something that they have to learn; it is not something that comes naturally. Most horses learn this at birth or shortly after, but some must learn this later on in life.

As riders, we don't *just* want to interact with the horse. We want to sit on his back. Every instinct of the horse tells it not to let a predator on its back. Through consistent, repetitive training, a horse can learn to trust humans enough to allow them on his back.

Again, horses are prey animals. This means that they are constantly on guard for danger. They view every new thing as potentially life threatening. Someone once asked me in reference to a horse that had never been handled by people before, "What reason does she have not to trust people?" However, the question in the horse's mind is, "What reason DO I have to trust people?" Until a horse finds an answer to this question, he will always be fearful. A horse's instinct when he is fearful is to run away. If he can't run, then he will fight.

However, horses can be taught to overcome their flight instinct. Through patience, kindness, and repetition a horse can be taught to deal with his fear in a different way. If you've seen a horse spook before, you know that it is usually an unpleasant experience for both the horse and rider, or handler. Luckily, there are ways that you can diminish the chances of your horse spooking by building up his trust and confidence.

Emotions cause us to react instinctively. We react with anger, fear, envy or frustration which often leads us into saying or doing things we later regret. Through training (studying the Word, praying, seeking God, fellowshipping) we can reprogram ourselves to react with kindness and love.

If a horse can overcome his instincts, so can we!

In much the same way we teach a horse to trust us and overcome his flight instincts, God will teach us to overcome our emotions and become more like Him. He will guide us and direct us. He will help us to get through new situations and show us how we can use those experiences to grow into better people. He will never give us more than we can handle with His help, so long as we continue to trust in Him and be obedient to Him. As we continue to walk with Him, our faith will grow, and we will learn to trust where He is leading us, just as the horse learns to trust his rider to safely guide him.

One thing you can be sure of is that God has your best interests in mind and His plans for you are good.

We are going to take a look at the story of a young girl named Esther to see just how things can work out when we trust the path that God has put us on.

The book of Esther is interesting because it is the only book of the Bible in which God is never mentioned by name. So why is it even in the Bible? Even though God's name never appears, it is easy to see His hand working throughout the story to bring about the desired outcome resulting in the Israelites being saved from a massive genocide.

The Book of Esther opens up with King Xerxes banishing his queen from Persia because she refused to attend one of his parties. The Queen had refused to obey the command of the King and so she was banished. A new queen was needed. All of the young maidens of the city of Susa were rounded up and brought to the palace, including Esther. Now, Esther was actually a Jew living in Persia. She and her people were exiles from Jerusalem and were treated as lower class citizens beneath the native Persians. So, in order to protect herself, Esther kept her true identity a secret.

I can only imagine what it must have been like for Esther to be taken from her family and stripped of everything she had once known. This was not a Cinderella story of women attending a ball in the hopes of wooing the prince. These girls were forced into service and became the property of a king with the power to banish them in an instant for any reason.

Each of the young maidens were taken before the king to see who he would choose. When it was Esther's turn, she found favor with the king and was chosen as the next queen. The Bible doesn't go into detail on what Esther's thoughts were at this point, but we can only guess that she must have been quite terrified. There was now no chance of returning to the life she had once known, she must keep her identity a secret, and she must live knowing that the last queen had been banished simply for not wanting to go to a party.

Not long after Esther was appointed queen, her cousin Mordecai, who worked in the palace, became aware of a plot to kill King Xerxes. Mordecai alerted Esther. She was able to make the plot known to the king, thus saving his life. Mordecai and Esther had found favor with the king.

The king's right-hand man was named Haman. Haman was a very prideful man and commanded all of the people of Persia to bow down before him. Mordecai refused to bow to this man, saying he would only bow before God. This angered Haman so he devised a plot to kill not just Mordecai, but all of the Jews. He tricked the king into signing a decree that all the Jews in the land were to be killed. Great mourning spread throughout Persia that day.

Mordecai went to Esther and told her of the decree and of Haman's evil plan. He begged Esther to go before the king and plead for the salvation of the Jews. This was the only way to save their people.

Esther, remembering the banishment of the former queen, replies "All the king's officials and the people of the royal provinces know that for any man or woman who approaches the king in the inner court without being summoned, the king has but one law: that they be put to death unless the king extends the gold scepter to them and spares their lives. But thirty days have passed since I was called to go to the king." (Esther 4:11) Esther knows that the king has a temper and that disobedience is not taken lightly. She is rightfully afraid of entering his inner court uncalled for. This could be a death sentence for her.

Mordecai responds, "Do not think that because you are in the king's house you alone of all the Jews will escape. For if you remain silent at this time, relief and deliverance for the Jews will arise from another place, but you and your father's family will perish. And who knows but that you have come to your royal position for such a time as this?" (Esther 4:13-14)

Mordecai is reminding Esther that God has a plan for her and that she needs to put her trust in Him despite her fear. God has allowed her to become Queen for a reason. Esther replies, "Go, gather together all the Jews who are in Susa, and fast for me. Do not eat or drink for three days, night or day. I, and my attendants, will fast as you do. When this is done, I will go to the king, even though it is against the law. And if I perish, I perish." (Esther 4:16)

And so, Esther, Mordecai, and all the Jews in Susa prayed and fasted for three days. Let's pick up the story in Chapter 5 to see what happens next.

On the third day, Esther put on her royal robes and stood in the inner court of the palace, in front of the king's hall. The king was sitting on his royal throne in the hall, facing the entrance. When he saw Queen Esther standing in the court, he was pleased with her and held out to her the gold scepter that was in his hand. So Esther approached and touched the tip of the scepter.

Then the king asked, "What is it, Queen Esther? What is your request? Even up to half the kingdom, it will be given you."

"If it pleases the king," replied Esther, "let the king, together with Haman, come today to a banquet I have prepared for him."

"Bring Haman at once," the king said, "so that we may do what Esther asks."

Esther had found favor with the king and her life was spared. She proceeded to prepare a feast for

Haman and the king. Let's continue the story in Chapter 7:

So the king and Haman went to Queen Esther's banquet, and as they were drinking wine on the second day, the king again asked, "Queen Esther, what is your petition? It will be given you. What is your request? Even up to half the kingdom, it will be granted."

Then, Queen Esther answered, "If I have found favor with you, Your Majesty, and if it pleases you, grant me my life—this is my petition. And spare my people—this is my request. For I and my people have been sold to be destroyed, killed and annihilated. If we had merely been sold as male and female slaves, I would have kept quiet, because no such distress would justify disturbing the king."

King Xerxes asked Queen Esther, "Who is he? Where is he—the man who has dared to do such a thing?"

Esther said, "An adversary and enemy! This vile Haman!"

Then Haman was terrified before the king and queen. The king got up in a rage, left his wine and went out into the palace garden. But Haman, realizing that the king had already decided his fate, stayed behind to beg Queen Esther for his life.

Just as the king returned from the palace garden to

the banquet hall, Haman was falling on the couch where Esther was reclining.

The king exclaimed, "Will he even molest the queen while she is with me in the house?"

As soon as the word left the king's mouth, they covered Haman's face. Then Harbona, one of the eunuchs attending the king, said, "A pole reaching a height of fifty cubits stands by Haman's house. He had it set up for Mordecai, who spoke up to help the king."

The king said, "Impale him on it!" So they impaled Haman on the pole he had set up for Mordecai. Then the king's fury subsided.

Haman's evil plan is averted, Esther finds favor with the king and all the Jews, and Mordecai is promoted to the king's second in command.

Looking back on the story, it is easy to see how God arranged the events to bring about the best outcome. Esther, a Jew herself, was chosen as queen. Then God allowed her to find favor with the king by exposing the plot on his life. Because of this, the king was welcoming to her when she entered the inner court. If Esther hadn't previously found favor with him, this could have gone very differently. Because Esther trusted in God throughout, she found the favor she needed, as well as the courage she needed to save her people. I'm sure there were many times where she was confused and scared and didn't understand why things were happening to her the way they were. God had a great plan for her all along. She just had to follow His leading one step at a time, trusting that He knew where they were going even if she didn't.

Sometimes what we ask our horses to do is hard for them. They may not understand what we want or why we want them to do certain things. They get confused and sometimes worried. They are challenged and through the challenges they grow and learn. It's not always easy, but what they don't know is that we have a plan for them, just like God has a plan for us.

I often feel like God only reveals His plan to me one step at a time rather than showing me the whole path. It is up to me to take that step trusting that God will then show me the next one and the next one after that. In the same way that we ask our horses to trust our leading, we need to trust in God's leading, one step at a time.

CHAPTER FOUR:
ENJOY THE PROCESS

"Around here... we don't look backwards for very long. We keep moving forward, opening up new doors and doing new things, because we're curious ... and curiosity keeps leading us down new paths."
Walt Disney

Learning how to ride is a process

Equestrians must be willing to put in the time to learn how to ride. Too many people think they can jump on a horse and learn to ride in a couple of hours. It may be true that they can stay on a really calm, forgiving horse, but they will not have the balance and control of their body that is necessary.

This leads to banging on the horse's back and yanking on his mouth, which is incredibly uncomfortable for such a sensitive animal. Some horses will forgive this behavior and action, but many will not. It is important to learn to ride correctly, not just to be able to stay on. As the rider, this means becoming aware of what your body is doing and learning how to control each movement that you make. Easier said than done when you are sitting on top of a 1000 lb. moving animal.

Students at the Spanish Riding School, one of the top Equestrian Schools in the world, will spend a year or more riding on a lunge line every day, without stirrups, before they are ever allowed to touch the reins. This ensures that they have truly developed the balance and control necessary to effectively communicate with the horses. Learning to ride is a skill that takes a lifetime to truly master. It is a process of learning, improving, and changing that never really ends.

Training a horse is a process.

Training a horse correctly is something that takes a long time and a lot of patience. You must be willing to spend time with the horse, developing a relationship with him. This means not just riding, but spending time working on the ground with him to build trust and respect.

Training a horse is not just about learning the

mechanical process of applying certain aids in order to achieve certain results from a horse. A horse is not a robot that can be commanded as you will. A horse is a living, breathing creature with thoughts and emotions of his own. You must learn how to communicate with the horse in a way that he can understand, considering the horse's own feelings and desires, as well as each horse's individual physical limitations. Horses are incredibly sensitive to emotions and energy and will often times reflect our own emotions, whether good or bad.

Patience is very important when training a horse. It is difficult to teach a creature that you cannot speak with. It is a long, slow process that cannot be rushed, or you'll risk losing the horse's trust. Occasionally, a horse will do something wrong, most of the time it is because the trainer was not clear enough with him. However, on occasion, the horse is simply misbehaving. It is important not to get angry when this happens. You must learn not to take things personally. The horse isn't misbehaving because he dislikes the trainer or wants the rider to look bad.

It's the same in life. Sometimes bad things happen, and we don't understand why. We need to learn to accept them and move on. God isn't punishing us or trying to make us look bad. He certainly doesn't hate us. Life is much more pleasant if we look at it with patience and a sense of humor.

Learning to train horses is more than learning to

apply a series of commands. It is about learning how to connect with another living creature on a spiritual level. This connection is something that takes a lifetime to achieve. The true joy of training is in the work that we do and the time spent with our horses, learning and growing together.

Becoming a better person is a process.

Sanctification (fancy church word for becoming more like God) is a lifelong journey as we strive to become more like Jesus. It is something that will not be completed until we go home to be with Him, but we know that He is always working in us.

Paul states in Philippians 1:6 that "he who began a good work in you will carry it on to completion until the day of Christ Jesus."

God has begun a work of grace in you. Charles Spurgeon comments, "The work of grace has its roots in the divine goodness of the Father, it is planted by the self-denying goodness of the Son, and it is daily watered by the goodness of the Holy Spirit; it springs from good and leads to good, and so is altogether good."[4]

God will not give up on you. He knows that you are going to fail. He loves you anyway. He will not leave you. Working with horses can help us along the way, as they bring both our strengths and our weaknesses into the light and show us a better way to live.

Hebrews 12:2 describes Jesus as "the author and finisher of our faith". Jesus is with us, helping us through every moment of our lives. It is not always easy. It is not always pretty. But he is always there. Maturing in Christ takes time, energy, determination, repetition, patience, and focus. We can only truly find those things by turning to Christ and leaning on his strength and trusting that He will never leave us nor forsake us.

Take a look at Peter, one of my favorite characters in the Bible. Peter undergoes an incredible transformation as he walks with Jesus. When Peter, who at the time was named Simon, first starts following Jesus, he's a simple fisherman, uneducated, hot tempered, tends to put his foot in his mouth and has doubts and fears. Simon is quick to speak, but when things get tough, he's quick to run.

God had a plan for Simon that far exceeded anything he could have imagined. Simon could have lived an "okay" life as a fisherman, but by choosing to walk with Jesus he lived an incredible life as a fisher of men, changing the course of history.

When Jesus met Simon, He gave him the new name of Peter, which means the rock. At this point, Simon was anything but solid or stable as the name Peter implies. Jesus didn't focus on Peter's current flaws; He saw the potential in Peter. He saw the finished work that Peter was to become. Jesus knew the plan

He had for Peter's life. When Simon decided to follow Jesus, he became a new creation, therefore becoming Peter.

But the transformation was not instantaneous. Peter had many struggles as he walked with Jesus. Jesus didn't expect instant perfection. He didn't wait for Peter to get his act together before asking Peter to follow Him. Jesus knew that as Peter walked with Him, he would continue to grow into the person that God created him to be.

When we make mistakes, we need to look at ourselves as a work in progress and trust that God will complete the work He has begun in us until we become the perfect creation that He intended us to be. We won't all change the course of the history of our world like Peter did, but all of us can change the course of history for at least one person, most especially ourselves.

Sometimes we encounter people who don't believe in us and that can be discouraging.

When we first met Anna, she was twelve years old and had never been handled by a human before. She was dirty, her mane was filled with burrs, and her feet were horribly overgrown. She was not a pretty picture and was barely recognizable as a noble

Andalusian with impeccable bloodlines. Not only was she a mess physically, but she had never, in twelve years, been taken away from her mother so she was very anxious about separation. However, that was all about to change. Her owners could no longer afford to keep her, and she had nowhere else to go. We decided to take a chance on her, going against the advice of everyone we spoke with about Anna's situation.

We had to catch Anna by bringing her mom into the barn and letting Anna follow her lead. We were able to get a halter on her to teach her the basics of leading, using her mother as a guide horse. We still needed to get her off the farm she was living at and to a place where we could more easily work with her. That's when the real adventure began.

Leaving the farm she had grown up on and the horses she had known her whole life was a traumatic experience for Anna. She had to learn what it was like to live in a stall. We could not turn her out for several weeks because she would feverishly pace the fence line, not allowing herself to be caught. It took many more months before Anna would allow anyone, but Nicole or I, to approach her outside. In the stall, she would pace and kick at the door whenever another horse would walk by. We tried allowing her to have the top portion of her stall door open to allow her to see out, but it wasn't long before she discovered that she could jump, from a standstill, over the 4 ½ foot bottom portion of the door.

Over time, we taught her to accept a saddle and a rider and began her dressage training, but she still remained highly agitated and nervous at all times. She would spook without warning and bolted on more than one occasion.

Over and over we were told to give up on her, that she would never amount to anything, that no amount of work would fix her. We were told that we weren't capable of working with a horse like Anna and that we didn't know what we were doing. Nicole and I continued to press on, but we did not have the support of anyone. Friends should be your biggest fans and strongest supporters, but that was not our case. We still believed that we could help this horse. We knew we could find a way to get through to her.

Ever so slowly, Anna began to trust us and relaxed. The progress was slow, but it was there. Yet, the criticism continued to the point where Anna was no longer welcome at our barn despite the fact she was behaving quite well, even better than other horses at that barn. So, a year after we first took her on, we moved to a new barn. The change in Anna was dramatic and immediate. Away from those who did not approve of her or welcome her, Anna truly began to settle down and learned to trust even more. Her behavior improved so much that I was able to begin using her as a lesson horse, first for my advanced students, but quickly progressing to the point where I could trust her with beginner riders.

Anna is now my best lesson horse.

Anna's physical transformation has been quite spectacular as well. She's gone from a rundown, shadow of a horse to a graceful, athletic, Andalusian who is performing at the highest levels of dressage.

The horse that no one believed in, or even wanted to give a chance, has shown us just what a little bit of faith and a lot of hard work can do.

Sometimes when we begin following Jesus, people will question our actions, or try to discourage us from pursuing the truth. When someone begins following Jesus, it transforms and changes their entire life. These changes can make people that surround the new follower of Christ, uncomfortable. And so, these uncomfortable feelings will force others to stop us from being followers. Satan, too, will try to discourage us in any way he can. Satan most certainly does not want us following Jesus. There will be many critics. It will not be a smooth path, and every time we fail, there will be someone around to point it out. We will doubt ourselves. In fact, there have been many times we have considered giving up on Anna. We never did. We pushed on despite everyone around us telling us we were going to fail. All we had was a little bit of faith.

A little faith is *all* that we needed. God took our little bit of faith and turned it into something amazing. God knows that we don't have much to offer Him and that's okay. He doesn't need much. He just needs our hearts. If we can give Him our hearts, He will handle the rest. Have faith. If God cares enough to transform a lost, forgotten horse, then He certainly will transform us too.

Sometimes on your journey, things may not happen the way you think they should or as fast as you think they should. I've worked with challenging horses before. Ilustre and Anna both had their issues when they came to us and were quite a challenge to train. I've worked with stallions and stud colts, aggressive horses, fearful horses, and wild mustangs. But, Maia, has been the most challenging to date because she not only tested my knowledge and technical abilities, but she challenged the core of who I am. Maia brought out things in me that were buried deep, dark and ugly. My fear and anxiety, that I thought was hidden deep inside me, came out full force.

Maia came to me as a 6-year-old who had lived her life on hundreds of acres on a ranch in South Dakota. She had very little training- basic ground manners and a bit of riding. Her world completely changed the day she left her ranch and came to live with us in Wisconsin.

Maia is a highly sensitive horse and very insecure. She has a difficult time trusting people. She was easily spooked and would startle, spin, and bolt. Anything could set her off including a noise in the distance, the wind rattling the arena door, someone walking past, or sunlight dancing on the ground.

At first, I accepted this as her just being in a new place and having to adjust. No big deal. I had worked with nervous and untrained horses before, but Maia would not settle down. A month passed, then two, then several, and there was very little change in her. Things weren't progressing at the speed that I wanted them too. I pushed harder and worked her more often. Still, no change. I did more groundwork. Still, no change. I tried every training technique I could think of. Still, no change.

Some experiences with other horses I had had in the past planted a seed of fear in me and, unfortunately, that seed had been growing beneath the surface. These fears were fueled by anxiety that I've suffered from my whole life. Maia's extreme reactivity brought my unwanted seed out to full bloom so that I became extremely fearful of riding her. My fear only increased her fear. It got to the point where I gave up riding Maia and stopped spending time working with her altogether. I was very discouraged, and, for a while, I just gave up.

Luckily, God brought me back. Through a series of crazy and amazing events, which you'll read about later, God restored my faith in Maia, helping me start over with her. My fear was brought into the light and God showed me how to overcome it. It has been a journey that we are still on. It's not always easy. There are still days where I do want to give up. However, God has promised me that He is the

God who can break all chains. He has a plan and purpose for Maia and me. I just have to be faithful and keep going. I need to stop worrying about the destination and start enjoying the process.

One of my favorite parts of training horses and teaching riders is seeing them progress and achieve things they did not think that they could do. All of the little moments and daily interactions are just as rewarding for me as the big accomplishments. I think God gets the same pleasure watching us grow as people.

Our ultimate goal is to be just like Jesus. We are human, so it is a goal that we will never fully achieve while on Earth, but that is not important. It is the journey that brings us the joy that God has for us.

Do not get discouraged when times get tough. When you start to get discouraged, don't look at how far you have to go. Instead, look at how far you have come. When Ilustre and I first came together, we were both a mess physically, emotionally, and spiritually. I was far from God and on a downward spiral while Ilustre was traumatized by fear. It was pretty bleak. With God's help, we were able to overcome it all and our lives were transformed. Today, I am in a position where I have led a small group studies, have taught Bible classes at VBS, and taught girls ministries classes. I have even gone on a two-week mission trip to Thailand! Crazy, right?

Ilustre, who was once barely rideable, is teaching students the art of classical dressage. Anna, who was once wild and unhandled, is now my most solid lesson horse. Maia is learning how to trust, and though she will always be a nervous horse, she has learned how to keep her fear in check. We've all come a long way.

I looked at my horses the other night and wondered how we got to this place where we are today. There is, of course, only one answer; only one way we could have achieved what we have. The power of God working inside us, guiding us on our path. That is what brought us to this place. God is always working in our lives, though often it is only in looking back, that we understand just how good His plans for us have been and currently are.

So next time you face a new challenge in life, approach it with curiosity, look for the lessons, and keep moving forward, following the path that God has for you.

Life with horses, and life with God, is an amazing adventure.

CHAPTER FIVE:
OVERCOMING FAILURE

"In the depth of winter, I learned that within me there lay an invincible summer." Albert Camus, French philosopher

In the last chapter, I shared with you some of my struggles working with Maia- how she wasn't progressing as fast as I thought she should be and how I had basically given up on her. Fortunately for both of us, God is an expert at overcoming failures.

After working with Maia, for what I felt was far too long and achieving nothing (or at least that's what I thought), I gave up and stopped riding her. I had failed to train this horse. Have you ever wondered if your failures have messed up God's plans?

I've got good news for you... you are not that powerful! God will accomplish what He needs to in spite of your failures. After all, He already knows about each failure and he already has a plan to handle each one.

I was surfing Facebook one day and just happened to come across a post stating that Frederic Pignon and Magali Delgado, the founders of the show Cavalia, were going to be doing a one-time clinic in the United States, in Aiken, South Carolina to be more specific. What an incredible opportunity to learn from the people who had inspired me so much in my journey with the horses. At first, I thought I would just go to audit, rather than bring a horse. Anna had just given birth, Ilustre was getting too old to make a 16-hour road trip, and I wasn't even riding Maia at the time, but Nicole convinced me that I should apply to participate. After all, this really was a once in a lifetime opportunity. So, I sent in my application, figuring if I was selected at all, it would be for liberty work since I wasn't riding the horse I was applying to participate with.

A few weeks later I got a phone call. I had been accepted, but not for liberty like I thought, but, instead, for dressage with Magali. What followed next was an uphill battle against the enemy's determination to stop me. The devil does not want us to overcome our failures. He wants to keep us down in the dirt because then we can't do anything for God.

Right from the start, there were things against us that made me doubt that this was really what we were supposed to do. The clinic was the Friday and Saturday before Easter, meaning we would spend Easter Sunday driving back from Aiken. Really, God? You want me to miss church on Easter? The most important day of the year, and I'll spend it driving rather than serving and worshipping you? That doesn't seem right. (I've since learned that God isn't a rules lawyer so if you miss church sometimes it's okay. After all, both Jesus and the disciples broke the rules of the Sabbath on various occasions.)

Then, there was the financial aspect of this situation. Participating in the clinic was not cheap and of course there were the travel expenses that went along with it. It was early spring, and we were still recovering from winter, which is always the slowest time of the year, as well as the expense of recently having a foal born to us. Finances were tight, and while we were getting by, we didn't have a whole lot extra.

I stressed over the decision quite a bit, but at some point, I remembered to pray about it. After that, a confidence settled on me that I have rarely experienced before. I knew we were supposed to go to that clinic.

However, things really began to get tough. One morning, a few weeks before we left, I was backing our truck out of the driveway. When I hit the brakes, the truck kept going. Praise God that it happened on our quiet street and I was able to simply coast to a stop. Nicole took a look at it later that day and discovered a break line had gone out. So now we had another expense. Okay, we can deal with that. Nicole fixed the brake line, and everything seemed fine.

During this time, I had begun to ride Maia again and it was not going well. I had such a strong fear that I could barely function while riding her. Now to be clear, I was never in any real danger riding Maia. She was spooky and unpredictable but realistically, as a professional trainer, I could ride through anything she did. I would never encourage someone to ride a horse that would put them in danger. This was not the case in this situation. If you have a horse that you are struggling with, I highly recommend seeking help from a professional trainer so that everyone stays safe.

On more than one occasion, my ride with Maia ended with me having a panic attack. How could I possibly attend a clinic where I was supposed to ride this horse that I was so afraid of? What was I thinking? I felt broken and hopeless, but God came through. He gave me a loving wife who supported me, and He showed me through the power of His Word how to overcome my fears.

I remember one day in particular that God came through for me. I had music playing on my phone to help calm my nerves while I was riding. The song "Whom Shall I Fear" by Chris Tomlin, came on and the words reminded me that God, along with His army of angels, is standing with me and fighting for me. I have a mighty friend in Him.

I was reminded of Daniel praying and fasting for 21 days during which time, unbeknownst to him, angels were fighting against the demons that were planning evil for him. Daniel was faithful to keep praying even though it did not seem like an answer was being provided. (Daniel 10)

I knew in that moment that my answer was coming. I just needed to be patient and continue to be faithful in my prayer and in the work that I was doing.

Things did eventually begin improving with Maia just as we were approaching the time of the clinic. However, the struggle wasn't over yet. We found out a week before the clinic that the horse trailer we were planning on using would not be available. We put out a desperate plea to the boarders at our barn when one of them came through for us. We had a trailer to use. Right around that time, Nicole began working night shifts to take care of a sick horse and I was busy trying to get ready for the clinic while still running my business. We were both exhausted, but the end was in sight.

A few days before the clinic, the brakes in the truck went out again. More expense. But even worse was the stress of getting it fixed in time. Somehow, we did and early Thursday morning we pulled out of the barn with Maia in tow. It rained the entire way from Wisconsin to South Carolina taking our 16 hour drive up to 18. There was no stopping us now!

It's hard to describe in words the stress and exhaustion and struggle we faced in the weeks and days leading up to this clinic. Everything seemed to be against us. Strangely, the harder things got, the more confident I was that we were supposed to go. I guess I realized that this was a spiritual battle and if the enemy was trying this hard to stop us, God must have something pretty amazing in store for us. Once I realized that, I became determined not to let it stop me. Now, don't get me wrong, I worried a lot. I complained a lot and I stressed a lot. It wasn't easy and I was still human, but I kept pushing. With God's help, we made it to Aiken late Thursday night.

God moved powerfully at that clinic. Maia and I experienced an amazing breakthrough and accomplished far more than I ever thought we would. I still have a hard time believing that I was blessed with the opportunity to ride with Magali Delgado. And believe it or not, it wasn't a once and a lifetime chance after all. A year later, we hosted a clinic with Frederic and Magali right here in Wisconsin. God often uses our failures to bring about future blessings.

If God calls you to do something, there is nothing that can stand against that unless you allow it. Satan doesn't want you to succeed. He is going to do everything he can to stop you. He will only succeed if you let Him. If you stand firm on the promises of God, fix your eyes on Him, and let Him do the fighting for you, then nothing will overcome you. As the saying goes, stop telling God how big your problems are and start telling your problems how big your God is.

Peter failed big time. He did the very thing he swore to the Lord he would never do. He denied Jesus not once, not twice, but three times. He couldn't even stand up for Jesus to a mere servant girl. Then, Jesus was killed, and it was all over. Of course, we know that's not how the story ends but imagine it from Peter's perspective. He had no idea that Jesus was going to rise again. Such a thing was impossible! So, Peter had failed, and Jesus was gone. How devastating that must have been for Peter.

Little did Peter know that it wasn't over. It was far from it. Three days later, Jesus rose from the dead and Peter was given the opportunity to redeem himself. Let's take a look at this encounter between Peter and Jesus from the Gospel of John…

Simon Peter, Thomas (also known as Didymus), Nathanael from Cana in Galilee, the sons of Zebedee, and two other disciples were together. 3 "I'm going out to fish," Simon Peter told them, and they said, "We'll go with you." So they went out and got into the boat, but that night they caught nothing.

Early in the morning, Jesus stood on the shore, but the disciples did not realize that it was Jesus. He called out to them, "Friends, haven't you any fish?"

"No," they answered.

He said, "Throw your net on the right side of the boat and you will find some." When they did, they were unable to haul the net in because of the large number of fish.

Then the disciple whom Jesus loved said to Peter, "It is the Lord!" As soon as Simon Peter heard him say, "It is the Lord," he wrapped his outer garment around him (for he had taken it off) and jumped into the water. The other disciples followed in the boat, towing the net full of fish, for they were not far from shore, about a hundred yards. When they landed, they saw a fire of burning coals there with fish on it, and some bread.

Jesus said to them, "Bring some of the fish you have just caught." So Simon Peter climbed back into the boat and dragged the net ashore. It was full of large fish, 153, but even with so many the net was not torn. Jesus said to them, "Come and have breakfast." None of the disciples dared ask him, "Who are you?" They knew it was the Lord. Jesus came, took the bread and gave it to them, and did the same with the fish. This was now the third time Jesus appeared to his disciples after he was raised from the dead.

When they had finished eating, Jesus said to Simon Peter, "Simon son of John, do you love me more than these?"

"Yes, Lord," he said, "you know that I love you."

Jesus said, "Feed my lambs."

Again Jesus said, "Simon son of John, do you love me?"

He answered, "Yes, Lord, you know that I love you."

Jesus said, "Take care of my sheep."

The third time he said to him, "Simon son of John, do you love me?"

Peter was hurt because Jesus asked him the third time, "Do you love me?" He said, "Lord, you know all things; you know that I love you."

Jesus said, "Feed my sheep. Very truly I tell you, when you were younger you dressed yourself and went where you wanted; but when you are old you will stretch out your hands, and someone else will dress you and lead you where you do not want to go." Jesus said this to indicate the kind of death by which Peter would glorify God. Then he said to him, "Follow me!"

Peter had not spoken to Jesus since before the crucifixion, since he had denied him. Peter now had a choice to make. He could let shame and fear control him and run and hide from Jesus (think Adam and Eve), or he could face Jesus knowing he had failed. Peter chose the latter, and Jesus welcomed him with open arms. Jesus did not condemn Peter. He did not scold him or tell him he couldn't be a disciple anymore or banish him from His sight. Instead He welcomed him and gave him the opportunity to redeem himself. Three times Peter had denied Jesus. Three chances Jesus gave him to reconfirm his love.

Peter would go on to fearlessly proclaim the Gospel and bring thousands of people to salvation. His work would change the course of history. Imagine how different things would have been if he had given in to shame and fear.

God will help us along every step of the way. He knows we are not perfect. He knows that we have no hope of being successful without Him. He is always there for us. We just need to be willing to accept his help. Failures are going to happen, but God will help us overcome them.

CHAPTER SIX:
FREE WILL

"The horse has such a docile nature that he would always rather do right than wrong, if he can only be taught to distinguish one from the other."
George Melville

"If a horse becomes more beautiful in the course of his work, it is a sign that the training principles are correct." Colonel Podhajsky

In riding, there is a term called self-carriage. Self-carriage means that the horse is carrying himself in a balanced and athletic position in which he is able to effortlessly perform whatever the rider asks of him. In order to do this, the horse needs to shift his weight onto his hindquarters, lift his back, and round his neck, therefore bringing his head down. This is a natural position that the horse will adopt all on his own when he is playing or showing off. The goal of training is to teach him to adopt this position when asked and to be able to consistently maintain it. This is important because self-carriage is the best position for a horse to be in in order to carry a rider. When the horse's neck and back are round it creates a stronger platform for the rider to sit on and allows the horse to carry the weight effortlessly. If the horse's head comes up, it causes his back to hollow which will put strain on his back, causing tension throughout his entire body. Over time, this can cause damage to his back, neck, and joints.

It's called self-carriage because the horse holds himself, choosing from his own free will to carry himself in that posture. He is not forced into position through tight reins, harsh bits, or other mechanical devices. If force has been used, then it is not truly self-carriage but an artificial position that is actually harmful to the horse. The horse should have the option not to do what we want but he chooses to anyway because, through correct training, we have shown him that what we are asking him to do is going to make him feel better.

Learning to live the Christian life is similar to the horse learning self-carriage. Like the horse, we are learning to behave in a certain way. This behavior is innate inside each one of us. It is there, hidden below the surface, buried under the cares of the world and the lies of the enemy. But it is there. Through gentle guidance and direction, God is able to bring it to the surface and transform us into a new creation. He takes the behaviors that are already inside of us (because He put them there) and grows and develops them into maturity. This is something that cannot be achieved by using force, or it will create resistance.

I happened to have been in the arena one day while a young girl was taking a lesson with her horse. She and her trainer were working on teaching the horse flying lead changes and were having some difficulty. The trainer made the statement that the horse "always gets angry first when we teach him something new, then he gives in." The sad reality is that this trend in the horse's behavior comes not from laziness or disrespect as many people would assume. Horses are actually very willing creatures and will generally try to do what is asked of them to the best of their abilities. This horse's behavior is a result of him, time and again, being forced into doing something that he is either not ready for, physically or mentally, or simply does not understand. This has caused this horse to become fearful whenever something new is asked of him, which results in him behaving defensively. Most people view this defensive behavior as disrespectful and so they turn to force to get the horse to do what they want. This only furthers the cycle of fear.

The problem is that most people don't take the time

to put themselves in the horse's place, to consider what the horse may be feeling. When a horse resists what you are asking of him, you need to stop and consider why he is resisting rather than just forcing him to do what you want.

Is he in pain? Pain should always be ruled out first. There are a variety of things that can cause a horse discomfort such as poor saddle fit, teeth problems, injuries, digestive problems, and more. It is important to work with a good vet to eliminate any physical problems.

Is the horse physically capable of doing what you are asking?

Does he understand what you are asking?

How are you asking? Are you asking with kindness and patience? Or are you demanding and harsh?

Here are some thoughts from dressage trainer, Jenny Rolfe, on this subject:

We need to listen to the horses in our care, ensuring that their behavior never becomes a plea for our help and understanding. If we can undertake the responsibility of fairness and consideration, we will be able to maintain a dialogue of 'communication' which does not lead to a dictatorship.
It might seem the easy option, or a quick fix, is to beat a horse into our way of thinking, but we can end up becoming desensitized to our own actions.

The response of the horse to continual harassment will, in time, make him become desensitized to the human. He may appear to cooperate, but his soul and individual personality will become soured, and his movements will become mechanical. His heart will not be in it!

This is the discipline for us, as we cannot successfully master a horse until we can become the master of our own personality. This is why Classical horsemanship takes a lifetime to achieve. The path is sound and all who follow this route can learn more of the fundamental qualities, missing from our way of life today.

Delfin (Jenny's horse) has taught me to continually be prepared to learn more and to be open minded in our work. I have also learnt that human nature is never 'all knowing' and we need to let go of our ego and allow the spirit of the horse to reach out and communicate with us.

I once thought that teaching the horse was about learning and refining the tools of training. The lessons I have learnt, however, since being part of Delfin's life, have a much more profound value. True horsemanship demands time, patience and a painful honesty, as our horses start to reflect us, and become our mirror. We may come face to face with behaviour which may be less than kind, confident and wanting to please.

There is a saying, that when we devote ourselves to God's creation, such as farming the land or caring for all creatures, then we are, in turn, brought nearer to our own Creator. [5]

God does not force us to do anything. He always gives us the choice.

Why did God give us free will? Because He loves us. God is all powerful. He could have forced us to obey Him. He could have forced us to follow Him. He could have forced us to worship Him. That wouldn't be love though. True love must be freely and willingly given. God desires nothing less from His beloved creation. He gave us free will so that we could freely return His love.

God *is* love. God loves each and every one of us with an everlasting love. God has a plan for each one of us. He knows that because of our poor choices we are destined for sin and hell. However, He has given us a way out. God loves us so much that he sent His only son to die on the cross for our sins, so that we might have eternal life with Him. All we have to do is choose to accept the salvation He has given us.

God will never force us to do anything. He simply invites us to let Him into our lives and allow Him to guide us and direct our paths. Following Jesus means giving up control of your life and giving it to Him. Remarkably, it is in this that we find freedom. Freedom from sin. Freedom from guilt. Freedom from worry and stress. We must make this choice on our own.

God will guide us. If we begin to go off course, He will use a variety of means to try to redirect us (His Word, others, things we read or see, etc.).

C.S. Lewis addresses this idea so simply yet perfectly in his book *The Magician's Nephew*.[6] In this scene, the two children, Digory and Polly, along with Fledge the Pegasus, have just been sent on a mission from Aslan (who represents Jesus). The day is drawing to a close, they are tired and hungry, and they have just discovered that they do not have anything to eat.

"Well, I do think someone might have arranged our meals," said Digory.
"I'm sure Aslan would have, if you'd asked him," said Fledge.
"Wouldn't he know without being asked?" said Polly.
"I've no doubt he would," said the Horse (still with his mouth full). "But I've a sort of idea he likes to be asked."

God is a gentleman. He does not force us to love Him or to follow Him. He simply offers us His love.

We have a choice to follow God and submit to his desires for us or to rebel and follow our own path. God loves us and wants what is best for us. His plans for us are good. He knows that turning away from Him leads to destruction, but He will never force us.

If a man is righteous and does what is

> *lawful and right….he shall surely live,*
> *says the Lord GOD….The person who*
> *sins shall die….But if the wicked turn*
> *away from all their sins…they shall*
> *surely live; they shall not die.*
>
> *…*
>
> *Have I any pleasure in the death of the*
> *wicked, says the Lord GOD, and not*
> *rather that they should turn from their*
> *ways and live?… Cast away from you*
> *all the transgressions that you have*
> *committed against me, and get*
> *yourselves a new heart and a new spirit!*
> *Why will you die, O house of Israel?*
> *For I have no pleasure in the death of*
> *anyone, says the Lord GOD. Turn, then,*
> *and live. (Ezek. 18:5,9, 20, 23, 31-32).*

God takes no pleasure in seeing people perish. He desires all to come to Him and be saved. We know love cannot be forced. And so, He guides us and pursues us with His love, and allows us the choice to come to Him.

God is always pursuing us with His love. He sends us love notes every day if we pay close attention. God's love is in the beautiful sunrise, the chirping of the birds, the kind word from a stranger, the child's laughter, the right song on the radio at just the right moment, the warm breath of your horse, the smell of fresh hay, and in so many other ways.

I remember one day, I was driving and was upset about something (I don't honestly even remember what it was). I looked up and saw a cloud in the perfect shape of a heart and felt God's love for me. Another time, driving and upset once again, I remember hearing in my heart God whisper His love for me.

Another time, I was nervous about speaking in front of our church. On the drive down all of my favorite worship songs played on the radio, as if God had picked them out and arranged a mix tape just for me.

One occasion that stands out to me, occurred several months before my mission trip to Thailand. This is while I was struggling to decide whether to go or not. Going to the other side of the world with a bunch of people I didn't know was terrifying for me, but it was something that I just couldn't get out of my mind. It was an absolutely crazy idea. At this point, I hadn't told anybody that I was considering this trip. I knew that once I started telling people, it would become more real and not something I could just ignore. I was struggling to work up the nerve to talk to Nicole about it. I was feeling scared and confused, and even a bit paralyzed. I didn't know how I could move forward with this. Then, in my heart, I felt a calming touch and I heard God whisper to me "even if you don't, I will still love you."

Those simple words broke the spell of fear that had

been paralyzing me. It was God's incredible love, that even if I failed Him, He would still love me, that gave me the courage to do what He was asking. He didn't ever force me. He just pursued me with His love.

In horse training, we attempt to guide and direct the horse so he performs a certain maneuver. If he goes off course, we need to redirect him so he can be successful. If we treat the horse with kindness and love, he is sure to want to follow us. If we try to force something, he will become resistant and unhappy and may rebel against us.

God loves us so much that He left heaven, came to Earth to be with us, and then descended into the depths of hell to save us. Now He lives with us, and in us in the form of the Holy Spirit, and He pursues us daily with His love.

It is His love, not any kind of force, deception, or trickery, that draws us to God and helps us to walk out the plans He has for us.

CHAPTER SEVEN:
SURRENDER

"When fear gets the best of me, I surrender to love." Unknown

Surrender is not something that is appealing to most people since we like to be able to control things. Surrender sounds like a negative thing. It sounds like giving up or losing. Surrendering to God is different. It is good and it leads to blessings, growth, and a deeper relationship with God, but it can be hard.

It is much easier to control a horse through force than to develop a partnership and simply trust the horse is going to do what you ask. People often try to control a horse's every move and reaction rather than allowing the horse the freedom to express his mood and desires. Horses that are never given the opportunity to say no are much easier to control than horses that are given a choice. But the relationship is much more fulfilling when the horse is your partner, not your servant.

It is much easier to have a god you can control, such as an idol, like your job, or money, or possessions, or to have a religion based on whether you prayed the right prayers, tithed enough and go to church every Sunday. It is easier to have a god who has very rigid rules to follow than it is to have a living, moving, unpredictable God who calls you to trust Him, and asks you to do things that don't always make sense.

In John 4, Jesus speaks with a woman at a well (breaking the rules by speaking to a woman, and even worse a Samaritan) and tells her, "Everyone who drinks of this water will be thirsty again, but whoever drinks of the water that I will give them will never thirst again. The water that I will give them will become in them a spring of water welling up to eternal life."

This is God's love for us. It fills us to overflowing and never runs dry. It is powerful and life changing. God's love is no small trickle. He lavishly pours it into us in a steady stream that will never run dry. As we are continuously filled, living water will flow from us to others around us. As we give it out to others, He fills us all the more.

Living water can be terrifying. It can't be contained or controlled. It's not predictable. It takes us out of our comfort zone. It requires us to surrender to God and to trust Him with our lives. It requires us to do things that don't make sense and sometimes even break the "rules".

Often times we try to replace this uncontrollable God with something of our own making. It could be anything such as money, power, relationships, possessions, work, or just a god who is predictable and contained. Anything that we feel like we can control.

Jeremiah 2: 11-13 states:

Has a nation ever changed its gods?
(Yet they are not gods at all.)
But my people have exchanged their glorious God
for worthless idols.
Be appalled at this, you heavens,
and shudder with great horror,"
declares the Lord.
"My people have committed two sins:
They have forsaken me,
the spring of living water,
and have dug their own cisterns,
broken cisterns that cannot hold water.

The people had abandoned the living water of God in exchange for broken cisterns of water. These cisterns are flawed for sure, but at least they can be controlled; they are predictable, familiar and comfortable. The people choose these over the powerful, living water of God.

These things will only ever be broken, flawed, and unable to truly satisfy us. On the other hand, God's love exceeds anything we could expect or imagine, and it's always freely given. Only God can satisfy our longings. We may try to fulfill our needs through other ways, but we are only wasting our time. We chase after things of this world when all along, God has so much better waiting for us if we would just turn to Him.

There was a time when I was beginning to feel empty. Business had taken over my life and I wasn't feeling as close to God. I felt like the work I was doing wasn't bearing any fruit and that I was failing Him. One Sunday, our pastor gave a beautiful sermon on seeking God first in everything you do. I was moved to the altar and spent time in prayer, begging God not to leave me where I was, but to transform me into the person He created me to be.

Later that day, Nicole and I attended a Christmas service with a friend at a church that easily sat thousands of people. We sang a few carols and then watched a video based on a quote by C.S. Lewis from his book Mere Christianity:

Imagine yourself as a living house. God comes in to rebuild that house. At first, perhaps, you can understand what He is doing. He is getting the drains right and stopping the leaks in the roof and so on; you knew that those jobs needed doing and so you are not surprised. But presently He starts knocking the house about in a way that hurts abominably and does not seem to make any sense. What on earth is He up to? The explanation is that He is building quite a different house from the one you thought of - throwing out a new wing here, putting on an extra floor there, running up towers, making courtyards. You thought you were being made into a decent little cottage: but He is building a palace. He intends to come and live in it Himself.

The speaker then went on to describe a house damaged by a flooded basement and my thoughts turned to our own recently purchased house which, at that very moment, had a basement covered in water. The house the speaker described wasn't left that way. It was repaired and restored until it was better than it had ever been. And so it is with us. God moves into our hearts and repairs and restores us.

Right there, in that room full of thousands of people, God spoke to me in such a deeply personal way, filled me with His love, and refreshed my spirit. It was an answered prayer made possible because I chose to surrender my hurting heart to the Great Healer and Restorer.

Whenever we feel dry and empty of God's love, we need only turn to Him, and by His deep love and immeasurable grace, He will fill us anew.

Surrendering is hard for us and it's hard for our horses.

I was working Maia in the round pen one day in attempt to have her stand still to be saddled. Maia did not want to have a saddle on her back despite the fact that she had been saddled many times already and knew the saddle wasn't going to harm her. She chose to run around the outside of the round pen rather than stand in the center with me and the saddle. She didn't know it, but she was her own worst enemy. She wanted to do things her own way, but this made everything so much more difficult for her. She was working hard by running around, but at any time she could have chosen to accept the rest I offered. All she had to do was surrender her own will and accept the saddle.

It made me think how, as humans, we so desperately cling to our own independence and our own ideas and desires. We are our own worst enemies. We make everything harder for ourselves. I was not trying to harm Maia or force her to do my will. I was trying to show her a better way to live. By accepting my leadership and allowing herself to trust me, Maia would be able to relax and let go of her fears. She could develop a partnership with me and allow me to meet her needs rather than trying to manage on her own.

God is not trying to harm us or to force us to do His will. He loves us more than we can even understand. He wants us to follow Him because He knows he can offer us a better life. He can give us rest. He can take away our fears. He can give us purpose. We have a choice. We can keep striving to do things on our own, our own way, or we can let go and let God take control.

I think of the disciples on the boat in the middle of the Sea of Galilee during a terrible storm, and yet Jesus is there out on the waves calling them to Him. Often, we cling desperately to the boat that we are in when Jesus calls us to step out onto the waves with Him. But the waves are dark and unpredictable and can't be controlled. That terrifies us. The boat offers security and familiarity and a sense of control, so we plant ourselves inside of it, refusing to budge. Here's the catch- the boat that we've made for ourselves will never stand up to the waves. Sooner or later it will be overcome, and it will sink, giving us over to the very waves that it was supposed to protect us from. The only way to truly stay safe is with Jesus. We need to leave the imagined security of the boat and step out onto the waves to be with Jesus and the true safety in Him. Jesus is sovereign overall and as long as we stay with Him, we will not be overcome.

———————

When training a horse to be ridden, one of the first things you need to teach them is to move forward when asked. Without forward momentum, it is very difficult to accomplish anything else. Without movement, it is impossible to guide or direct the horse. Without movement, the horse is much more likely to get himself into trouble. A horse that is not moving is more likely to lose focus and get distracted by the things around him; he's more likely to be tempted to misbehave and more likely to find something to be afraid of. As soon as he learns to move forward, under the direction of the rider, his focus improves, his mind turns to his work instead of the distractions around him, and he is able to be guided.

Our walk with Jesus is the same way. We need to learn to move at the guidance of our Lord. Sometimes we feel like we want God to tell us exactly what He wants us to do. We want all the details lined up and a flashing sign before we'll take a single step forward. God doesn't often work that way. When you ask a horse to move forward, he has no idea where you are going to take him. It could be around the arena or down the road or down some foreign trail he's never seen before. You may ask him to go over jumps or around poles. He has no way of knowing. He simply has to trust you to guide him through every step of the journey.

Most times God doesn't show us His whole plan. He just shows us the step right in front of us. We have no idea where He is going to take us. We just have to trust that He will guide us through every step, and He will get us to where we need to be.

God can't guide us if we aren't willing to move, to take that first step, even though we don't know exactly where we are going. We need to be willing to move and trust that God is going to guide us, otherwise we risk getting stuck in one spot. We risk getting ourselves into trouble. When we aren't moving, it is easier to get distracted by the worldly things around us and lose our focus on God. It is easier to fall into temptation and sin. It is easier to give into fear. As soon as we learn to move under the direction of our Father, we are better able to focus on Him. Our mind turns to Him and the work He has for us instead of all the distractions around us. God is then able to guide us.

Don't wait for God to make you move. Start moving and trust that He will guide you on the path He has for you. Just as the horse learns to move forward at the request of the rider, we need to learn to step out in faith when God calls us.

The Message sums up the words of Paul in Ephesians like this:

In light of all this, here's what I want you to do. While I'm locked up here, a prisoner for the Master, I want you to get out there and walk—better yet, run!—on the road God called you to travel. I don't want any of you sitting around on your hands. I don't want anyone strolling off, down some path that goes nowhere. And mark that you do this with humility and discipline—not in fits and starts, but steadily, pouring yourselves out for each other in acts of love, alert at noticing differences and quick at mending fences. (4:1-3)

The second thing a horse must learn is to stop and stand still when asked, without fidgeting or getting impatient. Sometimes God does ask us to just stay still and rest or wait for His timing for something. There is a difference between doing things for God and just doing things to do something. As we learn to recognize the difference, we will see that times of stillness are also a part of His plan. Asking a horse to stop and stand still can keep him from getting ahead of you, moving too fast or in the wrong direction, or it can help him to relax and refocus. For the same reasons, God may ask us to stop for a bit. Perhaps we are trying to get ahead of God and figure things out without listening to His direction. We may be moving too fast or in the wrong direction. Maybe we've lost our focus and are doing things for the wrong reason. Maybe we just simply need a break. These times of being still are important. At some point, God will ask us to start moving again.

Surrendering to God means moving when He asks us to move and being still when He asks us to be still. It means we listen to His guidance rather than trying to figure out everything on our own. It means we learn to let go of our problems and trust Him to take care of us. It means we will be taken out of our comfort zone, for it is there that the magic occurs. Our fears decrease and our faith is strengthened, and real change takes place in us and those around us.

Obedience is a choice we will have to make as we surrender ourselves to God's plan for us.

In Exodus chapters 11-12 we read the story of the Passover. Moses, speaking for God, has made many attempts to convince the Pharaoh of Egypt to free the Israelites from the bonds of slavery they have been under for hundreds of years. Pharaoh has refused, despite the many miraculous signs Moses has performed. Pharaoh's stubbornness and refusal to listen and obey led God to send the angel of death to claim the first-born child of every family, sparing the families of the Israelites, His chosen people. However, in order to be saved from the angel of death it wasn't enough to just be an Israelite. They had to prove they were obedient servants of the Lord by sacrificing a lamb and spreading the blood of the lamb across the door frame of their home. This was a choice they had to make. If they didn't obey, they wouldn't be saved.

Jesus has made the ultimate sacrifice for us. He was obedient to the Father to the point of death on a cross and thereby has cleansed us of all sin. Now we have a choice to make. Will we believe in Jesus and follow Him? It is not enough that we are Christians if we are not obedient to Jesus' commands to love God and love each other. Following Jesus requires action on our part. Our lives must be changed. We must turn away from sin and worldly desires and follow Jesus, allowing Him into our lives and giving Him our heart. Only then, can we be saved.

I have a young Arabian gelding in training with me right now. The other day, I was working on getting him used to being in the wash rack and getting rinsed off. He was nervous about standing in the confined space and decided to make his opinion known by attempting to run me over and escape. I had to show him that even though he was nervous, he still needed to respect my leadership and do what I asked to the best of his ability. I wasn't looking for perfection, but I was looking for him to at least try to be obedient. What he learned was that things really aren't that scary and that I would take care of him, as long as he listened and did what I was telling him.

It is the same way with God. God will ask us to do things that take us out of our comfort zone and how we react is important. Do we start kicking and screaming and resisting? Or do we trust God and try to be obedient?

After the young horse discovered that the wash rack wasn't so bad, he began to trust me more and became willing to try other new things without so much of a fight. Each time God calls us farther and farther out, it increases our trust for Him.

Obedience is especially hard when God's path for us is difficult and doesn't make any sense.

My wife, Nicole, is transgender. When we started dating it was Nate that I fell in love with. I married my husband. When Nate first came out to me as transgender, and began the transition to Nicole, I was faced with rethinking everything I believed about my life and our marriage. Though the church had always taught me that transitioning genders, along with same sex marriage, was wrong and sinful, it was something I very rarely thought about at all, and certainly not something that I ever thought would affect my life. For quite some time, I was very angry with God for putting us on this path and for the suffering that Nicole had already gone through. I was angry for the struggles we would continue to have to go through. This was not at all the direction that I wanted to go. This was not at all how I saw our marriage going. This was not a part of *my* plan for my life. Not too many people are prepared to find out that their spouse is not exactly who they thought. I never imagined myself going through this. Following this path would mean defying what the church told us was right and wrong, it would mean losing friends, and it would challenge my identity of myself as a heterosexual person and the fantasy image of the marriage I wanted. Not exactly a fun looking path. And so, I was angry, scared, and confused.

I spent much time in prayer and study, learning about what being transgender really means. I basically knew nothing, and the church had given me a lot of inaccurate information. As it turns out, the Bible is not as clear on the issue as some people seem to think. The verses that are often used to condemn homosexuality have been misinterpreted. Those verses were directed at acts of pagan worship, that don't resemble the loving, committed relationships of LGBTQ people. After prayer, and a lot of time to heal, I finally accepted the path that was before us. Once I did, I felt such a sense of peace and comfort. The Bible says that God gives a "peace beyond understanding" (Philippians 4:7) and that was exactly what happened for me. When God puts you in a situation that is beyond your understanding, He will give you a peace that is also beyond understanding. Nothing is beyond understanding for God.

Sometimes God calls us to do things that just don't make sense. This really shouldn't be a surprise to us since God does tell us "For my thoughts are not your thoughts, neither are your ways my ways... As the heavens are higher than the earth, so are my ways higher than your ways and my thoughts than your thoughts." (Isaiah 55:8-9)

Since then, my relationship with God has changed. He took me through some very dark times, and while we still have not come to the end of the struggles, I am beginning to understand the path. Through this, I have learned what it is like to be broken and an outcast. This has given me a much deeper compassion for all of God's lost children, something that I may not have otherwise learned.

Pete Buttigieg said it best in his speech to the

Human Rights Campaign, "The more you know about exclusion, the more you think about belonging."[8]

Because of our struggles and the exclusion we've faced, I have a greater empathy and desire to help all excluded people, even if they have been excluded for different reasons.

I don't know the end of our path, but I hope that the compassion that I'm learning for all of God's children will help make the difference in someone's life. It never would have happened if I hadn't made the choice to surrender to God's will for me, even when it didn't make sense.

CHAPTER EIGHT:
MIRRORING

"The horse is a mirror to your soul. Sometimes you might not like what you see. Sometimes you will."
Buck Brannaman

A client had been working with her horse for a few months doing liberty work with him. In this time, he had transformed from a disrespectful troublemaker into a well-mannered member of society. He learned to come when called, walk and stop with her, and to respect personal space.

I'm always up for a challenge so we decided to take both the other horse and my mare, Maia, into the arena at the same time, with the goal being for us to each work our respective horses at liberty at the same time.

The horses had never met each other so we started off by turning them both loose in the indoor arena and stood back to let them interact. What followed was quite interesting. Maia initially completely ignored the other horse and walked away from him without any acknowledgement. The other horse followed her. Maia continued to walk around, exploring the arena, and he continued to follow right behind her. When Maia stopped, he stopped. When Maia turned, he turned. When Maia walked or trotted, he followed suit. Maia eventually allowed him a brief greeting but was quick to end it and continue her exploration of the arena with him mimicking her every move.

Why is this significant? Maia, by ignoring him and walking away from him, had established her leadership and he, by following her, was acknowledging that he accepted her leadership and was willing to trust her. All of this happened within seconds. How? These two horses had never met before. How did they establish their roles so quickly and why was the other horse so willing to blindly follow a horse he had never met before?

Horses naturally seek to be around other horses and, when they are together, it is important to know who the leader is. The leader is responsible for directing the other horses' movements and keeping them safe.

In turn, the other horses are responsible for always keeping an eye on the leader so they know when it is time to move and when it is ok to stop. Now, here's the part that might surprise you- horses don't want to be the leader. Being the leader is a huge responsibility and all horses will gladly turn that role over to someone else, as long as they know that that someone would be an adequate leader. In the absence of someone they feel fits this requirement, they will assume the role of leader in order to protect themselves. Horses will fight to determine who would be the better leader, but oftentimes fighting is not necessary with one horse quickly submitting to the stronger leader.

The two horses were able to sense each other's energy levels immediately. Maia could tell that the other horse was too laid back to challenge her, so she immediately took leadership by walking away from him and he immediately chose to accept by following her. This happened exceptionally quickly in this case, but usually takes longer with the horses greeting each other and perhaps challenging each other to access each other's strengths and weaknesses.

So why does any of this matter?

What's interesting is that over time a horse will almost always mirror the personality of its owner. Just as the other horse was mirroring Maia's movements, horses will learn to mirror their owners and will even take on the personality traits of their owners. Confident owners have confident horses. Fearful owners have fearful horses. Disrespectful people have disrespectful horses. Stressed people have stressed horses. Angry people have angry horses. Content people have content horses. Happy people have happy horses. And so on.

If we let them a horse can open our eyes to issues in our lives that we need to deal with such as fear, hurt, or anger. Whatever we give to our horse, the horse gives back to us.

Horses imitate their leaders just as we are called to imitate and become more like Christ. We recognize that Jesus is stronger than us and we make a choice to follow Him and imitate Him.

So, what was important to Jesus? What does imitating Jesus look like?

"A new command I give you: Love one another. As I have loved you, so you must love one another. By this everyone will know that you are my disciples, if you love one another." (John 13:34-35)

Jesus is our role model and Jesus was all about love and kindness.

I was having a conversation with a client regarding her horse's behavior. This particular horse had been off of work for a year while his owner was pregnant. She was now desiring to start riding him again and wanted to address some issues she had

had with him in the past. She admitted to me that she thought his behavior was rude and he was being a jerk. The horse was poorly behaved, for sure, but I asked her to consider things from his perspective. We were trying to teach him something that he didn't know how to do. It was challenging for him both physically and mentally. He was worried because in the past he had been disciplined for doing the wrong thing without ever being taught what the right thing was. Imagine trying to figure out how to solve a complex problem while someone who speaks another language stares at you and gets upset every time you make a mistake. This would put a lot of pressure on you, make it difficult for you to concentrate, and create a huge amount of anxiety. The horse doesn't understand why we are asking him to do what we are. He doesn't know what the goal we have for him is. He just knows that his body feels strange and he's trying to understand what we want. If instead of seeing his misbehavior as him being a jerk, we see it as him struggling with something, we are going to act with much more empathy. We are going to encourage him to do the right thing rather than disciplining him for doing the wrong thing.

When the horse is encouraged, he will stop feeling like he needs to defend himself. He will start listening better and doing what is asked of him, even if he doesn't always understand. He will try harder. He will learn to relax and even enjoy the work that he is doing.

It is the same with the people around us. We are so busy that we don't even notice them most of the time. When we do, we choose to complain, argue, and gossip. We call people lazy, rude, stupid, and worse, without ever wondering what they might be going through.

In a world where mass shootings occur way too frequently, where entire groups of people are treated like outcasts because of who they are, where hurt and fear and brokenness are all around us and people are too busy to care, we could use a little more empathy and encouragement. We need to stop arguing with each other on social media. We need to stop blaming others for our problems. We need to stop sending thoughts and prayers without being willing to actually do something to make a difference.

James 2:14-17 says, "What good is it, my brothers and sisters, if someone claims to have faith but has no deeds? Can such faith save them? Suppose a brother or a sister is without clothes and daily food. If one of you says to them, "Go in peace; keep warm and well fed," but does nothing about their physical needs, what good is it? In the same way, faith by itself, if it is not accompanied by action, is dead."

So, what can we do? The answer is quite simple, and yet very difficult. The answer is simply having a little more empathy for people and encouraging them as much as you can.

How do you change the world? One act of kindness at a time.

Say hi to someone you don't know. Give someone a compliment. Take the time to notice when someone is struggling with something. Reach out to that person who hasn't been to church in a while. Sit with the kid who always eats alone at lunch. Notice the hurting and the broken. One act of kindness at a time.

Invite someone to church. Lend a listening ear. Send a card or a note letting someone know how important and special they are to you. One act of kindness at a time.

Share the gospel. Make a meal for the new mom. Visit with the lonely widow. Mentor the lost teenager. Play with your kids. One act of kindness at a time.

Stop arguing. Stop complaining. Stop gossiping. Stop bad mouthing individuals and entire groups of people. Stop judging. Stop assuming. Start accepting people for who they are. One act of kindness at a time.

Start loving people like Jesus did and try to see them through His eyes. Try to understand what they are going through. Do something to make them smile. To encourage them. To serve them.

One act of random kindness at a time and we can change the world.

Bob Goff says it quite simply- "The best advice I've ever been given when I failed- was a hug."

Jesus is our standard and our example in how to live. 1 John 2:6 says, "Whoever claims to live in him must live as Jesus did."

And John 12:15 says, "I have set you an example that you should do as I have done for you."

We should not compare ourselves to the world or live by the standards of the world. Just because a person says something is ok or acceptable to do, does not mean that it is. We need to look to God's Word to see what is acceptable. We live in a world where people lie, cheat, steal, and deceive to get ahead. Is this how we should act as well? After all, everyone else is doing it.

Standing up for what is right can be difficult at times, especially when we are the only ones doing it. It can make us very unpopular. When I decided to start standing with the LGBTQ community, I lost close friends and an entire church community. The disciples were ridiculed, tortured, and killed for standing up for their beliefs.

There is a lot of bad horse training out there. Unfortunately, in this day and age the focus has become training horses as quickly as possible, using whatever means necessary, to be able to succeed competitively. Bad training is rewarded in the show ring. There are also those who don't bother to invest in learning or training themselves or their horses. They settle for the bare minimum when it comes to their own abilities and what they've taught their horse. Either way, the cause is a lack of patience and work ethic to take the time to properly train their horses, and the horses suffer because of it, both physically and emotionally.

I have a book called *Grace for the Moment* by Max Lucado[9]. It has a different inspirational message for each day of the year. One message really hit home with me so I will share it. It talks about how change starts with each individual and how you should do what is right even if others aren't.

Do what is right this week, whatever it is, whatever comes down the path, whatever problems and dilemmas you face- just do what's right. Maybe no one else is doing what's right, but you do what's right. You be honest. You take a stand. You be true. After all, regardless of what you do, God does what is right: he saves you with his grace.

So, here is my challenge for you. Do what is right. Do what is right for your horse. Be kind to him. Eliminate forceful training. Teach him to perform through kindness, respect, and love. Sure, there are many people out there using forceful training methods and seeming to get great results. It would be easy to follow in their footsteps. But what about the horse? His spirit is broken. His mind is destroyed. This is not right. There is a better way, maybe it is not so easy, but it is better. Training through patience and love will create a horse that is truly your partner.

Next time you see someone being judged, ridiculed, or harassed stand up for them. Reach out to the outcast. Share God's love with the broken. What a difference we could make in the world if we simply do what is right.

One act of kindness at a time.

CHAPTER NINE:
FOCUS

"The successful warrior is the average man, with laser-like focus." –Bruce Lee

There are many distractions in this world that draw us away from God. We are easily drawn away from God with things like materialism, temptations, business, and more. We become focused on ourselves and what we want, forgetting about God. Sometimes we do the right things for the wrong reasons.

There was a time where I was going through some personal struggles and I didn't feel as close to God as I did when I first gave my life to him. I wanted to get that closeness back. I was running through things in my head, wondering what I was doing wrong. Am I not praying enough? Am I not reading and studying the Bible enough? Am I not serving enough? Am I not learning enough? Am I not surrendering enough? Suddenly it hit me. The phrase that I kept repeating… "am I not".

I was focusing on myself thinking of what I could do to earn God's love. As if I could ever hope to be good enough for God. I realized I need to stop focusing on what I am doing (not that those things aren't good) and remember that God's love is right there waiting for me. I don't have to earn it. In fact, I *can't* earn it. All I have to do is accept it.

People often lose focus of their horses as well. Horses live in the moment. They don't regret the past or worry about the future. When they are doing something (eating, resting, etc.) that is all they are thinking about. They are 100% present in the moment. They aren't thinking about what happened yesterday or what they are going to make for dinner later, or that rude thing that other horse did earlier. They are fully present in the moment.

When working with a horse, people must learn to be as equally present. Horses can tell if we are present or not. I know an old school horse who was a master at this. As long as his rider remained present and was actively riding him, he was a perfect gentleman, even with the most beginner of riders. However, the moment he sensed that his rider had mentally checked out, in other words was thinking about something other than what they were doing, he started making up his own agenda, which often meant a quick jump sideways leaving the rider in the dirt.

When working with horses, we must learn to put aside our worries, and simply be in the moment.

People can also lose focus when they become more concerned with doing well at a show than the well-being of their horse. People will push their horses to perform regardless of how it affects the horse. When this happens, people might turn to training methods that are damaging to their horses physically or mentally.

Horses can lose focus as well when their attention is on something other than the person they are working with. We've probably all worked with, or witnessed a horse, that was not paying attention to its rider or handler but rather focused on something else going in the moment.

When we lose focus, or our horses lose focus, things become a lot harder.

We need to keep our attention on God, and not just 30% or 60% or even 98% of the time. We need to fully commit to giving God our entire focus in everything we do, in every aspect of our lives. From our worship and prayer and Bible study, to our jobs, our time spent with our horses, cleaning house, grocery shopping, and every other mundane activity. When we fully devote our time to God, we will live a far richer life.

Earlier I talked about how my client and I had brought our two horses together to do liberty with them in the arena. Adding distractions such as other horses or food is a great way to test out your liberty skills to see where you still need to make improvements. Both horses had established a solid foundation of liberty work on their own, so now it was time to challenge them a little more.

We allowed the two horses time to meet and get comfortable with each other on their own terms, loose in the indoor arena. After a few minutes, it was time to test out our liberty skills. I called Maia and she came right over to me. This is the desired response, a horse that is obedient even with the distraction of another horse. I had worked with Maia with various distractions before, so she had learned how to keep her focus on me.

The other horse had other ideas. He continued to follow Maia around and refused to leave her when he was asked to. This shows that there is still some weakness in his partnership with his owner. He had not fully decided to allow her to be leader in every aspect of his life. He was perfectly fine following her when there were no other distractions, but as soon as he found something more interesting, he did what he wanted too.

With consistency and continued practice in a variety

of situations, they will have a much stronger relationship which will improve all of the work they do together.

Like the horse, there are many things in this world that can distract us, like that new car we want so we don't tithe or donate to the needy, the job that takes up our time so we don't pray, or even the worries and cares of the world that keep our focus on ourselves instead of our Creator.

If you've ever tried to accomplish something with a distracted horse, or teach him something, you know that it can be very difficult. First, you need to help the horse focus on you. Only then can learning and growth occur.

We, too, need to focus on God in order for Him to teach us and help us grow. It's hard to resist temptation and distraction, but luckily for us, we don't have to do it on our own.

Jesus understands our suffering and our struggles. Hebrews 4:15-16 tells us "…we do not have a high priest who is unable to empathize with our weaknesses, but we have one who has been tempted in every way, just as we are- yet he did not sin. Let us then approach God's throne of grace with confidence, so that we may receive mercy and find grace to help us in our time of need."

Jesus was tempted just as we are, but He was able to resist temptation using the powerful word of God and He gives us His example to help us in our own struggles. Let's look at Matthew chapter 4 to learn more.

Then Jesus was led by the Spirit into the wilderness to be tempted by the devil. After fasting forty days and forty nights, he was hungry. The tempter came to him and said, "If you are the Son of God, tell these stones to become bread."

Jesus answered, "It is written: 'Man shall not live on bread alone, but on every word that comes from the mouth of God.'"

Then the devil took him to the holy city and had him stand on the highest point of the temple. "If you are the Son of God," he said, "throw yourself down. For it is written:

"'He will command his angels concerning you, and they will lift you up in their hands, so that you will not strike your foot against a stone.'"

Jesus answered him, "It is also written: 'Do not put the Lord your God to the test.'"

Again, the devil took him to a very high mountain and showed him all the kingdoms of the world and their splendor. "All this I will give you," he said, "if you will bow down and worship me."

Jesus said to him, "Away from me, Satan! For it is written: 'Worship the Lord your God, and serve him only.'"

Then the devil left him, and angels came and attended him.

Jesus's temptation shows his humanity and provides us with a leader who understands our own suffering. Hebrews 2:18 says "Because He himself suffered when He was tempted, He is able to help those who are being tempted."

Jesus was first tempted with a physical need. He was hungry and so the devil asked him to turn stone into bread, something well within Jesus' abilities to do and something that would satisfy His hunger. Temptations often come in relation to our needs and desires. This could be physical needs such as food or clothing or money, or it can be emotional desires like the desire for respect or love or to be included. When we are tempted in this way, our trust in God to take care of us is called into question. If we don't have a strong trust, we will be more likely to give in to the temptation.

Jesus resists the temptation with the Word of God. Our spiritual strength from the Word is what gives us the ability to overcome the physical and emotional temptations. We must constantly fill up on the Word in order to stay strong. If we are spiritually empty, it will be easy for our physical and emotional needs to overcome us and lead us into sin. When we are spiritually full, we are able to stand up against these temptations.

The devil then tempts Jesus with doubt, calling into question who God said He was. The devil says *if* you are the Son of God and then tells Jesus to prove it. The devil knows that if he can get us to doubt then he can weaken our faith, therefore preventing us from following God's plan for us. Doubt is something that can start small, take root in our hearts, and then grow, taking over until it chokes out our faith. When our faith is weakened, we are weakened.

How can we overcome doubt? Jesus gives us an example. Once again, Jesus resists the devil's temptation using the Word of God. When doubt enters our hearts, we need to focus on the truth of what God says. This is why reading the Bible and knowing scripture is so important.

Once doubt enters our minds, it is easy for the devil to manipulate the truth to distract us from God, enticing us to do something we shouldn't. The devil encourages Jesus to throw Himself off the temple to prove who He is. Jesus is strong in His faith and firm in His knowledge of who He is, so He is able to resist this temptation. Adam and Eve weren't so successful.

Now the serpent was more crafty than any of the wild animals the Lord God had made. He said to the woman, "Did God really say, 'You must not eat from any tree in the garden'?"

The woman said to the serpent, "We may eat fruit from the trees in the garden, but God did say, 'You must not eat fruit from the tree that is in the middle of the garden, and you must not touch it, or you will die.'"

"You will not certainly die," the serpent said to the woman. "For God knows that when you eat from it your eyes will be opened, and you will be like God, knowing good and evil."

When the woman saw that the fruit of the tree was good for food and pleasing to the eye, and also desirable for gaining wisdom, she took some and ate it. She also gave some to her husband, who was with her, and he ate it. (Genesis 3:3-6)

The serpent is able to get Eve to question what God said. Once doubt has entered her mind, she is easily convinced to go against what God has instructed. This is why it is so important to remain focused on God and the Truth of His Word. We need to diligently study the Word so we can be confident in what God tells us about who He is, who we are in Him, and how we are to live our lives. So, for the second time, Jesus is able to resist temptation by staying focused and remembering the Word of God.

The devil had one more trick up his sleeve. His next move was to tempt Jesus with power and material possessions. This is one that many of us fall victim to. These temptations distract us from God and lead us away from Him. These temptations can be anything from money to work to success to power and to material things such as a new car or bigger house, or the coolest new technology. Anything that we desire can potentially lead us into temptation if we try to attain it by any means necessary. After the devil placed doubt in Eve's heart, he tempted her to eat the fruit by telling her that she would be like God. When we do things for our own gain, we are easily led astray.

It is so important to keep our focus on God. When we become distracted by things of the world, we are easily led into temptation. However, when we keep our eyes on Jesus, He keeps us on the right path.

For the third time, Jesus resists the devil with the Word of God and an important message for all of us. He says, "Worship the Lord your God, and serve Him only."

We need to fully submit all areas of our lives to God. Remember, Jesus lives inside of you and gives you the strength you need to resist. Galatians 2:20 tells us "I have been crucified with Christ; it is no longer I who live, but Christ lives in me; and the life which I now live in the flesh I live by faith in the Son of God, who loved me and gave Himself for me," and 1 John 4:4 tells us "You are of God, little children, and have overcome them, because He who is in you is greater than he who is in the world."

When you feel tempted, keep your eyes on Jesus, remember the Truth of the Word, and ask Him to help you. He will always help you. Hebrews 4:16 says "Let us therefore come boldly to the throne of grace, that we may obtain mercy and find grace to help in time of need," and 1 Corinthians 10:13 promises us "No temptation has overtaken you except such as is common to man; but God is faithful, who will not allow you to be tempted beyond what you are able, but with the temptation will also make the way of escape, that you may be able to bear it."

Temptation is something that we all face, but by keeping our focus on God, we are able to overcome and stay on the path that God has for us.

CHAPTER TEN:
SENSITIVITY

"Neither horse nor man likes anything in the world that is excessive." Xenophon

"Therefore keep watch, because you do not know on what day your Lord will come." Matthew 24:42

When a horse is focused on his rider, he is able to remain sensitive to the cues of the rider and is able to respond correctly, allowing himself to be guided through a seemingly invisible connection between horse and rider.

Horses are very subtle creatures. I was once doing a

groundwork demonstration with a horse in front of several people who had never worked with horses before but were interested in learning. One girl innocently commented that my cues were "too subtle", that she had a hard time seeing them. Well, she may not have noticed all of my cues, but the horse (who was doing everything I asked to perfection) certainly had!

Horses, as prey animals, are incredibly aware of everything that is going on around them. Small changes in physical position, along with mood or energy level, mean huge amounts to a horse.

One thing I've learned through working with horses, is that less is more. When you figure out how to do less (physically) then you will achieve more (partnership with the horse, horse becomes more expressive, gives you more). A good trainer learns to make every action mean something and not to do something without understanding why you are doing it. One must learn to listen to the horse.

Horses feel and respond to subtle changes in energy. They can tell the difference between someone who is positive versus negative, confident versus insecure. They can also feel differences between increased versus decreased energy. Riding teaches you how to do things through feel, how to use your intuition. You can have all the book knowledge in the world, but still not be able to ride. Riding teaches you how to get in touch with your body. By connecting with your horse, you are able to become better connected with yourself, and better connected with God. We are able to connect with God through His creatures.

Horses can become dull, though, through improper training. If a rider continuously uses heavy force when applying pressure to the bit, over time, the horse will learn to lock his jaw and brace against the bit in order to protect himself from the pressure. These horses are often termed "hard mouthed" because when pressure is applied to the bit, they resist it rather than giving to it. Unfortunately, many people try to "fix" this problem by using a strong or more severe bit to apply an even greater amount of pressure to the horse's mouth. This only causes the horse to brace further and become harder in the mouth, therefore bigger and bigger bits must be used.

The same is true of riders who improperly use whips and spurs to encourage their horses to go forward. Overuse of these tools will cause a horse to become "dead sided", ignoring the cues from the rider.

Eventually, if enough force is used, the horse will simply shut down. He may perform as asked but he will be lifeless and dull. He has mentally "checked out" in order to protect himself from the pain he is experiencing.

All of this could be prevented by proper training in which the rider is sensitive to the needs of the horse and does not use force to control the horse.

People, too, can lose their sensitivity. What once seemed so evil somehow becomes acceptable. We become dull to the enormousness of our sin. The Bible warns us of this…

They are darkened in their understanding, alienated from the life of God because of the ignorance that is in them, due to their hardness of heart. Having lost all sensitivity, they have given themselves over to sensuality so as to indulge in every kind of impurity, and they are full of greed. (Ephesians 4:18-19)

Paul warns the Christians of Ephesus not to become like the Gentiles who, because of their ignorance, have become hardened toward sin. Their feelings have been dulled so they no longer care if they are sinning or not. This leads them to sin all the more which, in turn, furthers the hardening of their hearts.

"Observe, when men's consciences are once seared, there are no bounds to their sins. When they set their hearts upon the gratification of their lusts, what can be expected but the most abominable sensuality and lewdness, and that their horrid enormities will abound?" (Matthew Henry)[9]

In today's culture, sin runs rampant. It is popular, it is accepted, even expected and sometimes encouraged. Lying, cheating, stealing, sexual immorality, substance abuse and more are things we face every day. You can't scroll through social media without seeing bullying, gossiping, name calling, and lying. Seeking power and wealth at any cost is encouraged and rewarded. It's easy to become dull to these things and begin to accept them.

On the other hand, hardness can also happen when we become too focused on the rules and forget about God's true calling for us which is loving one another. This is what happened to the Pharisees. These highly respected religious leaders knew the Torah (Jewish Bible) forwards and backwards, but they didn't understand anything about God's heart. They used their position of power to persecute and exclude certain groups of people. They would point out the sins of others while ignoring their own sins. They looked down on people who were different than they were. They ridiculed Jesus for spending time with people who were considered lower class. In the end, they called for the crucifixion of the Son of God.

This hardness can happen to Christians today as well. We become prideful in our beliefs and look down on those of other religions, or prideful in our country as we look down on people of other nationalities. We can judge others' sins while ignoring our own. Religion is used to manipulate and control people. Religion is used to exclude people and justify discrimination.

This hardness leads to people being excluded from the church and that is not God's desire.

We must remain sensitive, so that we always stay tuned to God's heart for us and for those around us.

To do this, we must stay in communication with God. The most important part of communication is listening. It's much easier to talk to God, to tell Him our needs and desires, but listening is even more important. We need to learn how to quiet our minds and open our hearts to allow God to speak to us.

God whispers to you in the dark. Can you hear it? Can you feel His presence surround you? If you are not paying attention, you might miss it.

I'd like to share a story straight from the Bible that shows what can happen when we aren't willing to listen.

Balaam got up in the morning, saddled his donkey and went with the Moabite officials. But God was very angry when he went, and the angel of the LORD stood in the road to oppose him. Balaam was riding on his donkey, and his two servants were with him. When the donkey saw the angel of the LORD standing in the road with a drawn sword in his hand, it turned off the road into a field. Balaam beat it to get it back on the road.

Then the angel of the LORD stood in a narrow path through the vineyards, with walls on both sides. When the donkey saw the angel of the LORD, it pressed close to the wall, crushing Balaam's foot against it. So he beat the donkey again.

Then the angel of the LORD moved on ahead and stood in a narrow place where there was no room to turn, either to the right or to the left. When the donkey saw the angel of the LORD, it lay down under Balaam, and he was angry and beat it with his staff. Then the LORD opened the donkey's mouth, and it said to Balaam, "What have I done to you to make you beat me these three times?"

Balaam answered the donkey, "You have made a fool of me! If only I had a sword in my hand, I would kill you right now."

The donkey said to Balaam, "Am I not your own donkey, which you have always ridden, to this day? Have I been in the habit of doing this to you?"

"No," he said.

Then the LORD opened Balaam's eyes, and he saw the angel of the LORD standing in the road with his sword drawn. So he bowed low and fell facedown.

Numbers 22:21-31

Balaam's heart was hardened so he was unable to see the angel standing before him. However, his donkey, who remained sensitive to God, *was* able to see the angel. The faithful donkey tried to warn Balaam. The donkey's behavior was unusual so Balaam should have recognized that something was wrong. Balaam was too focused on himself and his own plan that he missed the warnings God was sending him through the donkey.

This story is thousands of years old, but still today,

horses, if we allow them, can open our eyes and lead us to a greater understanding of life. If horses today could talk, I sometimes wonder if they would ask us why we don't just listen to them…why we choose to make things harder on ourselves through our stubbornness rather than being willing to learn a new way of doing things. The horse knows and sees the Truth and he can show it to us. Horses can show us both our strengths and also our weaknesses, and they can help bring about the changes that we need to find the happiness we desire.

Sometimes the answer we are seeking is right in front of us. We need only open our eyes, our ears, and our hearts to God's will for us. We need to put our focus on Him and remain sensitive to His will for us.

CHAPTER ELEVEN:
HUMILITY

"The horse, with beauty unsurpassed, strength immeasurable and grace unlike any other, still remains humble enough to carry a man upon his back". Amber Senti

"We have almost forgotten how strange a thing it is that so huge and powerful and intelligent an animal as a horse should allow another, and far more feeble animal, to ride upon its back". Peter Gray

"One reason why birds and horses are happy is because they are not trying to impress other birds and horses." Dale Carnegie

Caring for horses is a lot of hard work. The hours are long, and the work is physical. There are stalls to clean, feeding, watering, grooming, medical care to handle, fixing fences, stacking hay, and the list goes on. It is a 365 day a year job. Through the work you learn humility. You must be willing to humble yourself to serve another, in this case the horse. The horse needs this care from you and, as a horse owner, it becomes your responsibility. The horse is dependent on you to take care of him and provide for him. It is through this humbling work that you are able to develop a beautiful connection with your horse.

I wrote this poem one evening while contemplating some of the trials and joys of life on a farm.

Life on a Farm

1:00am.

Up late tonight with a colicky horse.

Talking to her, comforting her.

Praying for a miracle.

Mercury reads 17° on this cold winter night.

5:00am.

Morning chores begin.

Frozen fingers doling out grain, filling water buckets,

Cleaning out stalls, sweeping the aisle.

Life on the farm begins to stir.

12:00pm.

The sick horse is eating again.

Her eyes are alert, and her ears are relaxed.

She nickers a greeting to you and

The whole farm breathes a sigh of relief.

2:00pm.

An afternoon ride on the horse of your dreams.

The cold, crisp air brings him to life.

Shoulder-in, haunches-in, piaffe, passage,

The dance begins, two moving as one in harmony and joy.

5:00pm.

Evening grain to pass out,

Picking stalls again, does it ever end?

Pause a moment and listen.

Soft sounds of horses happily munching on hay.

9:00pm.

Final check on the horses.

Everyone is cozy and warm.

Then it's off to bed.

Counting your blessings, praising God, and looking forward to the next day.

Horses are very humble creatures. An average horse weighs approximately 1000lbs. His strength and beauty are immeasurable. He could crush us in an instant if he so chose. But he doesn't. Instead, he allows us to sit upon him and direct his movements, through the love and trust that he has placed on us.

Horses, unlike people, don't spend time comparing themselves to other horses or trying to be better than the other horses. They accept themselves as they are and live in the moment without dwelling on how they compare to the other horses around them.

A horse can tell the difference between a proud person and a humble person. A horse will often resist a person that is prideful but will forgive the mistakes of someone who is humble. The horse will often perform better for the humble person, even if that person has less skill, than for a more skilled but prideful person. Horses don't understand pride, don't feel comfortable around it, and therefore resist it. After all, to the horse, the prince and the peasant are no different.

All people are equal, no matter who they are, and a horse will perform no differently for someone simply based on who they are or some title that they have. It is only by humbling ourselves and providing the love and care that the horse needs and desires that we can truly develop a lasting relationship, bringing out the best of the horse's abilities. The more humble we are to our horse, the more he will be willing to try his best for us and the more he will give himself to us.

God also loves and honors humility.

The Bible has a lot to say about humility which shows us just how important it is. Humility is required for salvation, repentance, and in order to receive and give grace. Let's look at some verses in the Bible that talk about humility.

2 Chronicles 7:14: If my people, who are called by my name, will humble themselves and pray and seek my face and turn from their wicked ways, then I will hear from heaven, and I will forgive their sin and will heal their land.

Humility is a requirement for repentance. We must be willing to admit that we failed God and ask for His forgiveness. God is faithful and His promises are true. If we humbly admit our sin and turn away from it, then God will forgive us. There is no sin that is too large and no sin that is too small for God to forgive. God offers His forgiveness freely and to all. We need only be humble enough to ask for it. We must set aside our own self desires and make Jesus the most important thing to us. When we realize how much we are dependent on Him to live the life He has called us to, we are able to trust Him and be obedient to Him. If we are willing to humble ourselves, we receive the beautiful, powerful gift of God's grace.

Psalms 25:9: He leads the humble in what is right and teaches them His way.

God can only lead us and teach us if we are humble. A prideful person thinks they have all the answers and thinks they can be self-sufficient. They often refuse to accept instruction and especially correction. In order to learn and grow in Christ, you must be willing to humble yourself and admit that you don't know everything and that you've made mistakes and need God's help. A wise person knows that they do not have all the knowledge or all the answers. They are willing to accept help and are eager to continue learning and growing. God is able to use this willingness to draw us into a deeper relationship with Him and to lead us into the life He has for us.

Philippians 2:5-8: (Jesus) being in very nature God, did not consider equality with God something to be used to his own advantage, rather He made himself nothing by taking the very nature of a servant being made in human likeness. Being found in appearance as a man, He humbled himself by becoming obedient to death— even death on a cross!

Jesus is our ultimate example on how to live our lives. Jesus loved us so much that He was willing to humble Himself enough to leave heaven and become a man, to serve others, to take our sins upon Himself, to suffer and die for us.

Psalms 149: 4: For the LORD takes pleasure in His people; He adorns the humble with victory.

When we are humble and ask God for help, He gives us the strength to overcome the struggles in our lives. Our humility allows the Holy Spirit to work in us and through us, and to bring about the victory we are seeking.

Proverbs 11:2: When pride comes, then comes disgrace, but with humility comes wisdom.

Pride often leads us to act foolishly in order to preserve or promote our own reputation or to work for our own gain. However, when we remain humble, we are able to think and act wisely. God is able to teach and guide us in the right direction.

Proverbs 3:34: He mocks proud mockers but shows

favor to the humble and oppressed.

This proverb is so important that both James and Peter chose to quote it in their epistles (James 4:6 and 1 Peter 5:5). Pride puts a barrier in our relationship with God, just as it does in our relationship with our horses, but humility opens the door for grace and forgiveness. Just as a horse will resist an overly prideful rider and perform better for a more humble rider, God opposes the prideful and His blessings flow through the humble.

Mark 9:33-37: They came to Capernaum. When he was in the house, he asked them, "What were you arguing about on the road?" But they kept quiet because on the way they had argued about who was the greatest. Sitting down, Jesus called the Twelve and said, "Anyone who wants to be first must be the very last, and the servant of all." He took a little child whom he placed among them. Taking the child in his arms, he said to them, "Whoever welcomes one of these little children in my name welcomes me; and whoever welcomes me does not welcome me but the one who sent me."

Humility was important to Jesus as He lived a life of a servant to others. Jesus often spent His time with people who were looked down upon, or outcasted. He loves all His people equally. There are no outcasts in the Kingdom of God.

John 13:12-17: When He had finished washing their feet, He put on His clothes and returned to His place. "Do you understand what I have done for you?" He asked them. "You call me 'Teacher' and 'Lord,' and rightly so, for that is what I am. Now that I, your Lord and Teacher, have washed your feet, you also should wash one another's feet. I have set you an example that you should do as I have done for you. Very truly I tell you, no servant is greater than his master, nor is a messenger greater than the one who sent him. Now that you know these things, you will be blessed if you do them.

Washing feet was seen as a task for the lowliest of servants and yet Jesus, Lord of all Creation, humbled Himself and washed the feet of His disciples. Then He called them to do the same for others. We should all be servants to each other just as Jesus came to serve us.

Jesus calls us to imitate His example and be servants to others. This is how others will experience God's incredible love through us. God uses us to share His love through humble acts of kindness just as Jesus did.

Why is humility so important? When we become prideful, we put ourselves and our own desires above God and above the needs of others. Our focus becomes on ourselves. God wants our attention to be on Him, and rightfully so. After all, He is the one who created us, and He has our best interest in mind at all times. We may think we know what we need and want, but our focus is on our temporary, earthly happiness. God cares less for our temporary

happiness because His focus is on our eternal glory.
God has eternity in mind for us. He wants to do
everything He can to make sure that that eternity is
spent with Him. This may mean that, at times, He
needs to sacrifice our temporal happiness to ensure
the security of our eternity. A humble heart focused
on God will trust in Him and His plan and be able to
weather the temporary hardships. A prideful heart
will turn away from God. God knows how
important it is for us to keep our focus on Him.

Jesus, who was God, did not desire equality with
God. Rather, He humbled Himself, became man,
and became a servant to men. He humbled Himself
to the point of death on a cross. God raised Him and
exalted Him above all else. All will bow to Him.

Contrast that to Satan who became prideful (Ezekiel
28:12-17) and desired to be exalted above God
(Isaiah 14:13-14). Satan was thrown down by God
and will spend an eternity in torment, whereas,
Jesus is exalted and lifted up above all others. The
more humble you are the more you will be lifted up.

"The first will be last and the last will be first in the
Kingdom of Heaven." (Matthew 20:16)

Jesus set an example for us. God loves a humble
heart. All those who humble themselves before God
and men will be lifted up and exalted in heaven.
The more we are able to humble ourselves before
God and others the more we will strengthen and
deepen our relationship with God and our horses.

Jesus was willing to give everything up in order to be obedient to God and to bring salvation to His people. What a sacrifice He made for us. What sacrifice are you willing to make for Him?

CHAPTER TWELVE:
FORGIVENESS

*"He's not going to look back if you don't.... They're
the most forgiving creatures god ever made."*
Nicholas Evans

*"Grace draws a big circle around us and says we're
in." Bob Goff*

This was a hard chapter for me to write.
Forgiveness is hard. When someone hurts us, it is
only natural for us to feel angry, sad, frustrated,
bitter, confused. It is our mind's way of protecting
us from being hurt again. But holding on to those
negative feelings can actually lead us to more
suffering. Instead, we need to learn to let go.

Horses don't hold grudges. They forgive our

mistakes. They let things go and never dwell on the past. A youngster in the herd in his exuberance may be pestering one of the older mares. The mare will immediately let him know that his behavior is not tolerated by pinning her ears at him or, if necessary, kicking or chasing him away. However, as soon as the youngster responds to her by stopping the disapproved behavior, she will end her discipline of him. They will then both move on with their lives and can often be seen grazing side by side in perfect contentment. Two horses may be fighting over food one minute and then happily grooming each other the next minute. They don't hold grudges, or hold on to hurt feelings, or judge each other, or let pride stand in the way of a future relationship. They deal with the issue at hand and move on.

I've made many mistakes when working with my horses. I've been unfair to them, unkind to them, I've taken my emotions out on them, and I've asked them to do things for me that they should not have had to do. Each and every time my horses have forgiven me.

Making mistakes when working with horses is inevitable. It's a part of the learning process. None of us are born a perfect rider or a perfect horse person. We will do things wrong. There will be days when our actions cause the horse to feel confusion, or frustration, or maybe even pain. Despite our best efforts, there will be times when we screw up.

A horse knows your heart and they forgive those mistakes.

Each day is a new day and a fresh start with a horse.

If only we humans could learn to live like this, how much more peace would we have? Holding on to unforgiveness only hurts yourself. Over time, it will eat away at your happiness.

The Bible is full of examples of forgiveness. Here are just few:

In Genesis we meet a pair of brothers, Jacob and Esau. Esau was the elder brother and Joseph was jealous of the way their father, Isaac, favored Esau. Jacob devised a way to trick Esau out of both his inheritance and Isaac's blessing for him. When the plot was revealed, Jacob had to run for his life in order to avoid the consequences of his actions. Many years pass before the brothers meet again. When a time finally comes when Jacob cannot avoid Esau, he is terrified that his brother will still be furious with him. But Esau has no anger, only forgiveness, and embraces his brother warmly.

Later on, in Genesis we meet Joseph and follow his story as he is almost killed and then sold into slavery in Egypt by his jealous brothers. A series of crazy events leads Joseph from slavery to jail to becoming the second in command to Pharaoh. Famine strikes the land but thanks to Joseph's wisdom, Egypt has stored up enough food to endure the famine. Joseph's brothers come to Egypt, not knowing that Joseph is there, desperate for food and hoping to find help. Joseph could have easily turned them away. After everything they had done to him, certainly they didn't deserve his help. However, Joseph chooses to forgive them, healing and restoring their family.

David is known as a man after God's own heart, but David had his own failings. At one point in time, he committed adultery with one of his closest friend's wife, causing her to become pregnant. Afraid of what would happen and refusing to take ownership for his mistakes, David went on to orchestrate the death of his friend in attempt to hide the affair. God was furious with David and David faced some terrible consequences for his actions. When David finally admitted his failings and with a broken heart confessed before God, God forgave him.

David shows us that when we sin, there are consequences for our actions. Just because God forgives us does not mean those consequences will be taken away. But forgiveness always brings healing.

Jesus shares a parable, found in Luke 15, that is the perfect illustration of God's love and forgiveness for us.

Jesus continued: "There was a man who had two sons. The younger one said to his father, 'Father, give me my share of the estate.' So he divided his property between them.

"Not long after that, the younger son got together all he had, set off for a distant country and there squandered his wealth in wild living. After he had spent everything, there a severe famine in that whole country, and he began to be in need. So he went and hired himself out to a citizen of that country, who sent him to his fields to feed pigs. He longed to fill his stomach with the pods that the pigs were eating, but no one gave him anything.

"When he came to his senses, he said, 'How many of my father's hired servants have food to spare, and here I am starving to death! I will set out and go back to my father and say to him: Father, I have sinned against heaven and against you. I am no longer worthy to be called your son; make me like one of your hired servants.' So he got up and went to his father.

"But while he was still a long way off, his father saw him and was filled with compassion for him; he ran to his son, threw his arms around him and kissed him.

"The son said to him, 'Father, I have sinned against heaven and against you. I am no longer worthy to be called your son.'

"But the father said to his servants, 'Quick! Bring the best robe and put it on him. Put a ring on his finger and sandals on his feet. Bring the fattened calf and kill it. Let's have a feast and celebrate. For this

son of mine was dead and is alive again; he was lost and is found.' So they began to celebrate.

"Meanwhile, the older son was in the field. When he came near the house, he heard music and dancing. So he called one of the servants and asked him what was going on. 'Your brother has come,' he replied, 'and your father has killed the fattened calf because he has him back safe and sound.'

"The older brother became angry and refused to go in. So his father went out and pleaded with him. But he answered his father, 'Look! All these years I've been slaving for you and never disobeyed your orders. Yet you never gave me even a young goat so I could celebrate with my friends. But when this son of yours who has squandered your property with prostitutes comes home, you kill the fattened calf for him!'

"'My son,' the father said, 'you are always with me, and everything I have is yours. But we had to celebrate and be glad, because this brother of yours was dead and is alive again; he was lost and is found.'"

God is our heavenly Father and offers forgiveness to us gladly. He is always ready to welcome us with open arms and celebrate our return to Him. We have all sinned and we all fail God, but God is always ready to forgive.

Forgiving someone who has hurt you can be hard; it

can even seem impossible. We can find encouragement in the forgiveness that Christ has already given us. Paul tells us in Romans that Christ died for us "while we were yet sinners". That's right. He didn't wait for us to stop sinning and clean up our act, or make amends and pay restitution, or even to apologize. He died for us and thereby offered us forgiveness while we were *still* sinning. He offered His forgiveness to the people who turned against Him, to the disciples who abandoned Him, to the Romans who tortured and killed Him, and He offers it to you and me, though we still sin.

Jesus forgave the sinner on the cross and promised Him eternal life in heaven. This sinner was about to die and would never have a chance to change his ways or make amends for his sins. Jesus forgave him anyway. If Christ can do all that for us, surely, through His grace and strength, we can forgive those who have hurt us. When we do, we will find peace.

Sadly, forgiveness does not always mean that the relationship will be restored. I am working toward forgiving certain people who have hurt me, but I know that allowing them back into my life would bring more hurt since there has been no change in behavior. Because of this, I have had to make the decision to distance myself from them in order to protect myself. This does not mean that I can't or won't forgive them. Forgiveness is between you and God and is what allows you to heal from your hurt. While, in many cases, it also happens between you and the person who hurt you, sometimes that is not possible. Sometimes it is not wise, or even safe, to continue a relationship with someone who has hurt you. In this case, forgiveness happens in your heart.

Jesus offers His forgiveness and grace to each and every one of us. It does not matter what you have done in the past. Peter denied Jesus, the disciples abandoned Him, and Saul persecuted and killed the early Christians. Yet, each one of them was willing to humble themselves and ask for forgiveness. Forgiveness was freely given. Each one of them went on to serve God and do amazing work in His name.

Jesus died for us and for the forgiveness of our sins while we were still sinning. He didn't wait for us to get our act together. He didn't wait for us to ask for forgiveness. He didn't make us beg or plead. He knew that we would continue sinning. He knows we are not perfect. He died for us anyway. He forgives us anyway.

Jesus will forgive you. All you have to do is ask.

Jesus also instructs us to forgive others as He has forgiven us.

It is hard. So very hard. Some of our hurt runs very deep and it is not easy to let go.

As I am writing this, I am struggling with forgiveness.

When Nicole decided to transition from male to female, we were no longer able to attend the church that we had attended and faithfully served for the previous five years. I lost friendships with people that had been such an intimate part of my life. People that had once meant so much to me, no longer wanted to be there for us. It is unbelievable to me how quickly someone so close to you will turn against you. It seemed that nothing I had done in the last five years to serve and love this church mattered. In the months after leaving the church, I had people unfriend me on social media. Some people I have never heard from again. Others sent hateful messages. I was told God didn't love me and that I was going to hell and I was called a variety of colorful names, both privately and publicly, by people who I had once called friends and brothers and sisters in Christ. I've received more hateful messages from the people who claim love as their standard than from the non-believers in my life.

I am angry. Angry at the church for their treatment of the LGBTQ community and the horrible example of God's love they are portraying to the world. I am angry at the thought of all the people who will never know God's love because of churches that refuse to share it with them. I am angry at my once friends for abandoning me during a time when I needed them most. I am angry at how closed-minded people can be, and how unwilling they are to listen to a testimony they don't like, and how quick they are to abandon. I am angry at God for allowing this to happen.

But it is deeper than that. My anger is grief. I am heartbroken. I have been abandoned by some of the people I was closest with. I was turned away by the people who claim to welcome all, just as you are. The church is a place that is supposed to always be there for you, always love you. There were days when, in my anger and pain, I wanted to walk away from God and faith and religion completely. However, I know that you don't leave Jesus because of the failures of others. And, Jesus forgives.

Jesus knows what it's like to be hurt by those closest to Him. He was betrayed by one of His own disciples, one of His closest friends. He was sold out for 30 pieces of silver. What about His other friends? They abandoned Him at His darkest hour. Peter denied even knowing Him, not once, but three times. The people He had spent time with, teaching and healing, mocked Him, sentencing Him to death. The church that should have been glorifying Him, had Him killed.

Yet, He forgave them and offered His grace. There was no anger, only love. Peter, who denied knowing Jesus, was not cast out. No, he became pivotal in the forming of the new church and served God faithfully until his death. Saul, who persecuted the early Christians and had many of them killed, went on to spread the Gospel to people far and wide and his writings form a large part of the New Testament. How different things would have been if Jesus had refused to forgive Peter and Saul. So many good works would not have been possible.

One thing I've learned is that forgiveness is a choice you have to make and an action you have to take. You cannot just sit around and wait for it to happen on its own. It's not a feeling that will happen if you wait long enough. You need to choose to forgive someone. Oftentimes you will have to choose to forgive the same person over and over again as you continue to release the hurt that they've done to you. You may choose today to forgive and then tomorrow you are reminded of the hurt and must choose to forgive all over again. You must continue to choose forgiveness no matter how many times the hurt and anger tries to creep back in. This is the only way to find healing.

It is also something that we cannot do on our own. Our own human nature stands in the way. It is through the strength and love that Jesus fills us with that we are able to offer forgiveness even to the people who have hurt us the most.

Jesus loves us so much that He died a brutal death so that we might have eternal life and forgiveness and He offers us His strength so that we too may offer that forgiveness to others.

CHAPTER THIRTEEN:
AUTHENTICITY

"Horses do not live in fear of tomorrow's scarcity nor are their motives managed through guilt and do they do not question or have a need to dislike themselves. The absence of shame eliminates the need for lying or hiding their emotions, so what they feel on the inside is what gets expressed on the outside, even when that expression appears to be no expression." Terry Church

Horses, unlike humans, don't typically hide their emotions. Their actions reflect their emotions. Meaning, if a horse is afraid, he will act afraid; if he is frustrated, he will act frustrated; if he is content, he will act content. Of course, different stressors affect each horse differently based on the horse's individual personality. What causes fear or frustration in one horse may not necessarily cause those feelings in another horse. Some horses are more sensitive to stressors than others. That being said, once a horse feels a certain emotion, he will usually display it, though the signs can often be very subtle. Horses don't lie about, or try to hide their emotions, the way people sometimes do.

Unfortunately, there are people who try to repress any form of emotion in their horses. They see any kind of expression as misbehavior in the horse. Horses are punished for showing any kind of emotion whether it is happiness, playfulness, fear, confusion, or even pain. After time, these horses shut down mentally and no longer show any emotion. They become mechanized, almost robotic, in the way they perform. There is a dull look in their eyes as if there is no life left. They have given up.

This is what happens when emotions are suppressed. It happens to people too.

Horses are extremely sensitive to subtle changes in emotion (breathing, heart rate, energy level) which alert them to potential danger. As a prey animal, this sensitivity is vital to their survival. They can sense changes in not only in other horses but also in their human partners as well. These changes are often so subtle that they are not visible to the human eye. In her article "The Hidden Wisdom of Feeling" Linda Kohanov[10] describes a study that illustrates just how sensitive horses are to our emotions.

In a 2009 article published in The Veterinary Journal, researchers from the Swedish University of Agricultural Sciences performed a simple yet elegant experiment designed to study the effect a nervous handler has on the heart rate of his or her mount. Twenty-seven horses of various breeds and ages were led or ridden at a walk by 37 amateur equestrians. Wearing heart-rate monitors, each team traveled a 30-meter distance between two cones a total of four times. Just before the final pass, however, the person was told that an assistant, who had been standing next to the path the whole time, would open an umbrella as the horse went by.

As it turns out, those scientific pranksters didn't even open the umbrella (as any equine liability insurance company would be relieved to know). Even so, the heart rates of both human and horse rose significantly as they passed the now suspect, inclement-weather savvy lab assistant. Even more remarkable, no behavioral differences were observed in either horse or handler when the animal was being led, though there was a tendency for riders to shorten their reins after the dreaded news was conveyed. So, especially in the case of people leading their equine companions, the mere human thought of the umbrella's spooking power was enough to raise the arousal of the handler and consequently, almost simultaneously, the horse, who I'm pretty sure would not have understood the experimenter's warning in Swedish.

Horses are highly sensitive to our emotions but often become confused or frightened when we try to hide how we are feeling by putting on a mask. Humans often try to repress emotions rather than dealing with them and will act differently than how they are feeling. This is confusing to horses who are unable to separate emotions from behavior.

Kohanov goes on to describe this condition:

In order to survive, animals preyed upon in nature are highly sensitive to changes in the stance, heart rate and blood pressure of herd mates and predators at a distance. In the wild, for instance, horses, zebras and deer will often graze unconcerned as a lion who has recently eaten a big meal walks right through their pasture. Yet when an agile carnivore is on the prowl, the herd will scatter long before the cat can get so close.

The experience of living with human beings has given domesticated horses even more sophisticated skills. I've seen even the gentlest gelding become noticeably agitated when his handler wears a mask of confidence and well-being to hide anxiety. It's as if this person appears out of focus to the equine awareness system. The body language of someone "putting on a happy face" is incongruent with the rise in blood pressure, muscle tension and emotional intensity transmitted unconsciously by an individual who's actually afraid, frustrated or angry. ... A secure, well-cared-for animal will often relax the moment his owner simply acknowledges a hidden feeling—even if it's still there. Let me say it again: The emotion doesn't have to change in order for the horse to show at least some improvement. The handler just has to acknowledge what he or she is really feeling.

All you have to do to ease the tension in your horse is to honestly admit how you are feeling. You do not necessarily have to change the feeling but, by just being honest with yourself, you change your emotions enough that your horse can sense and respond to it.

Interestingly, this can also happen in our interactions with other people as Kohanov goes on to say:

Studies on the neurophysiology of emotion show that even human beings exhibit stress responses in the presence of incongruent people. In Social Intelligence: The New Science of Human Relationships, emotional intelligence pioneer Daniel Goleman cites research proving that not only does a person's blood pressure escalate when he tries to suppress feeling, the blood pressure of those interacting with him also rises. Basically, unless you're a sociopath, your blood pressure, heart rate, and breathing intensify when you're frightened or angry, even when you're wearing your best poker face. It takes extra energy to hide these feelings, which adds to the anxiety radiating from your body, through whatever complex process scientists are only now beginning to uncover.

In our human culture, emphasis has been placed on verbal communication so we have lost much of our sensitivity to the nonverbal messages we may be sending or receiving. It has become (or maybe it always was) common practice for people to hide or repress their emotions in an attempt to appear as though nothing is wrong and they "have it all together".

Unfortunately, this even happens in the Church. There is a lie that has infiltrated our lives and our community that says that once you come to Jesus you better get your act together and the sooner the better. God is up there in the clouds looking down on you, shaking His head. This lie causes people to hide their problems and to put on a mask. Someone asks how you are doing, and you retort "I'm fine", when deep down you are anything but fine. You feel like you can't let them know your truth. Being honest causes conflict, judgement, and anger. It is better to avoid all of that. It almost becomes a competition to see who can be the most perfect and happy. This is not the love Jesus called us to.

Sadly, people can be very judgmental. It can be hard to admit that you don't have it all together. It can be hard to trust people enough to open yourself up. Maybe you are hiding depression and pretending to be happy; maybe you are pretending to have certain beliefs or social status. Maybe you are hiding your sexual orientation or gender identity. Maybe you are afraid of something and don't want to admit it because you think people will accuse you of not having any faith. Maybe you've messed up and feel like you need to hide it, so no one knows that you've failed. Whatever it is, when you hide a part of yourself, it keeps you from the peace that comes with authenticity.

Being authentic is hard. It means taking risks and opening yourself up to being hurt by others. When Nate decided to transform into Nicole and live her life authentically as the person God created her to be, it was a difficult road. There was hurt and loss as others decided they didn't want to support her transition. But Jesus was calling to Nicole to leave the former self and step into her true identity as she was created to be. We were not created to live a lie and we were not created to live anything less than our true, authentic selves. This is the only way to true happiness.

When you repress your feelings, they never really go away. They are bubbling away below the surface just waiting for an opportunity to attack full force. Eventually they will come out and it usually gets pretty messy when they do. The more we repress things the stronger those things become. We may start off with feelings such as hurt or frustration, but these soon grow to anger, bitterness, fear, pride, and even hatred. When these feelings eventually do surface (which they will), you will have much bigger problems to deal with.

Jesus calls us to live authentically, truly loving others for who they are so that they, in turn, can truly love us for who we are. No pretending. No trying to impress each other. No secrets and lies. Just honest, heartfelt love for someone. This is the freedom that we find in Jesus.

It is hard to carry around the burdens of life on our own, to try to do everything in our own power. Jesus promises "my yoke is easy and my burden is light" (Matthew 11:30). When we are honest with God and honest with others about our problems, it allows God and others to share our burden. It breaks the chains holding us down along with the shame, anger, and possible guilt. It, instead, gives us love and grace. The only way to truly find freedom is to surrender your life to Jesus and embrace the love He has for you, that He has always had for you, just the way you are. True joy comes from being comfortable enough in your own skin to live your life honestly and openly, trusting in God, and living out of His deep love for you. Then, you too, will discover the "secret to being content in any and every situation". (Philippians 4:12)

Horses are able to express themselves freely without judgement. They feel no pressure to perform. They don't worry about what the other horses will think of them. Horses are able to experience true freedom and joy. They are able to be at peace with themselves.

We can learn so much from them. God wants us to be able to live our lives authentically as the person He created. He doesn't want us to hide His beautiful creation behind a mask. Our true beauty lies in our brokenness.

CHAPTER FOURTEEN:
UNCONDITIONAL LOVE

"The horse already knows who he is. Do you know who you are?" Unknown

One of the most beautiful things horses can offer us is a glimpse of what unconditional love is like. They don't care what we look like, how wealthy or popular we are, or what we have to offer them. They just love us. They are there for us on our good days and our bad days. They don't care if we put on make-up and wear the right outfit or say the right things. They simply enjoy being with us, just as we are. This bond we create with our horses runs deep and, for many people, gives them comfort and strength in this difficult world.

But as deep as our bond with a horse can be there is only one person who can truly
satisfy our deep need to be loved...Jesus.

God loves you. It is impossible for us to truly understand the love that God has for each one of us. God loves us so much that He sent His only Son to die a horrible death for us so that He could be with us. Our sin separates us from God, and it is only through the blood of Jesus that we can be with Him. God willingly made this sacrifice for us. Just think about that for a moment. Let it really sink in. God wanted to be with you so much that He let His Son die in your place. Jesus died for the world, but He also died for you personally. If you were the only person that could be saved by His death, He still would have willingly gone to that cross. This love is amazing in itself, but God didn't just leave it at that. He didn't just save us. He continuously and lavishly pours out His love on us as we go through our lives with Him.

Paul, in his letter to the Ephesians, wrote a prayer for those he was ministering that they might be able to understand the love God has for each one of them. Paul knew that God's love has the power to transform lives, to break chains and set people free, to give hope and peace and acceptance. Once you understand even a little of God's love for you, you will never be the same. So, this is my prayer, also, for each of you reading this, that you would be transformed by the power of God's love.

For this reason I bow my knees before the Father,

from whom every family in heaven and on earth is named, that according to the riches of his glory he may grant you to be strengthened with power through his Spirit in your inner being, so that Christ may dwell in your hearts through faith-that you, being rooted and grounded in love, may have strength to comprehend with all the saints what is the breadth and length and height and depth, and to know the love of Christ that surpasses knowledge, that you may be filled with all the fullness of God. Now to him who is able to do far more abundantly than all that we ask or think, according to the power at work within us, to him be glory in the church and in Christ Jesus throughout all generations, forever and ever, Amen. (Ephesians 3:14-21)

God's love is so incredible that I don't think we will ever really understand the fullness and depth of it until we get to heaven. It is just simply beyond our understanding. Maybe that's why God gives us horses, so that we can understand just a little more the unconditional love He has for us. Horses can help us on our path, giving us glimpses of the love God has for us.

They can also teach us lessons about how we need to love others.

———————

When Maia first came to me, she was fresh off a

ranch in South Dakota where she roamed free over hundreds of acres of land. She had had some handling when she came to me for training, and had even been ridden a few times, but she had never been away from that ranch in the middle of nowhere. At the time, our business was beginning to grow, so we decided to purchase Maia with the intent of training her to use as a lesson horse. She settled into her new home surprisingly well. The farm we were at was very quiet, so I guess it was enough like the farm she had come from to make her feel comfortable. Her training began. She was athletic and intelligent and within a few weeks she was able to walk, trot, and canter under saddle as well as perform some basic lateral movements.

It was then that we made the decision to move our business to a new barn. This was a much larger barn and we felt the move was what the business needed to continue in its growth. Unfortunately for Maia, another move, along with the fact that this new barn was so completely different from the ranch she had come from, was more than she could handle. She had gone from a quiet ranch in South Dakota to a bustling boarding stable in Wisconsin. There were people everywhere, dogs barking, strange horses, a large metal arena that made funny noises when the wind blew (which is quite often in Wisconsin), and cars driving by all the time. Inside the arena, there were things like jump standards, brightly colored barrels, horses and people coming in and out, doors that slammed shut in the wind, and four walls that limited her range of view.

All of this was too much for Maia. She became very fearful. She would spook at any little movement or noise. Sometimes it was all I could do to keep her from running around the arena in a blind panic.

I was disappointed. The horse that had initially progressed so quickly through her training and was well on her way to becoming my star lesson horse, was now virtually un-ridable. For a while, I tried to continue with her training, but she remained fearful. The more I pushed her to work through her fears, the more fearful she became.

I have worked with fearful horses before, from off the range mustangs to horses that had been neglected and abused. Typically, with enough time and patience, the horse would settle down and learn to trust. However, months passed, and I saw no change in Maia. I became even more disappointed and frustrated. This was not what I thought I was getting into when I purchased Maia. This was not the lesson horse I was looking for.

The next few months were busy with lessons, shows, and clinics. Maia's training was put on hold. When I did begin to work with her again, I decided to start completely over with her to see if I could rebuild a relationship with her. So, I went back to the very beginning with liberty work. The liberty work did wonders for building her confidence. At first something would scare her, and she would run away from me, but over time when something scared her, she would run *to* me. This showed a level of trust we had never had before.

I began to realize that I had created certain expectations from Maia that she was unable to meet. This led to disappointment on my part which prevented us from developing a good relationship. I was withholding my love from her because she wasn't following my timetable. I was never mean to her; I simply was holding back from giving her my whole heart. As long as I continued to expect things from Maia that she was not capable of giving, we continued to butt heads instead of learning to work together. However, once I let go of these expectations and decided to love Maia where she was, the barriers she had built up began to come down.

It's been a slow journey, but everyday Maia's confidence grows. As you read earlier, I was eventually able to start riding Maia and since that clinic with Magali, she has improved by leaps and bounds. I'm even using her for lessons now. She still spooks at things, but now instead of going into a blind panic, she stops and looks to me for guidance. Our relationship has grown so much deeper since I stopped expecting things she couldn't give me and started to just love her. We still work hard and push our limits, but I don't get disappointed in her when she fails. Failure happens to all of us. It's part of the learning and growth process.

I have no doubt that if I continue to love Maia just as she is and give her that time she needs, she will one day be a great lesson horse. But if not, that's okay too. I'm going to keep loving her right where she is.

God loves us just as we are. He doesn't need us to be perfect. He already knows we are not. He knows each one of our mistakes and failures before they even happen and yet He chose to die for us anyway. He welcomes us with open arms into His family. You don't need to wait until you get your life together to have a relationship with God. Start following God and He will help you get your life together. It's a journey that you walk with God, not something you have to do before you come to Him. He will walk it with you and help you every step of the way.

I have struggled with anxiety disorder for as long as I can remember. My anxiety tells me that I need to be perfect or I will fail. It tells me that others are constantly judging me, that I am not good enough. It tells me that I am unlovable. For so long during my childhood and young adulthood, I didn't realize that I had anxiety. I just thought there was something wrong with me. That me, at my core, was wrong, bad and unlovable. I hated myself.

Even with people I am close to, I have a hard time opening up and letting them really know me without feeling like they are judging me.

Horses gave me some comfort. Horses were there for me no matter what. I felt comfortable around horses because horses don't judge. Being around horses got me through some pretty tough times.

When I finally realized that I had this condition called anxiety it was a huge relief. I learned that there were other people out there who dealt with similar things that I had. It's an incredible feeling to learn that you are not alone. I was able to begin to figure out why I did certain things and why I reacted the way I did. I was able to learn to control my anxiety better. But I still hated myself and felt like my life was a mistake.

Around the same time, I went to a conference that would change my life. It was the Original Women's Conference held at City First Church in Rockford, IL. The theme of that year's conference was Ever and Always in reference to the love God has for us.

Jen DeWeerdt, the leader of the conference, opened up the weekend with a powerful sermon focused around the verse Jeremiah 31:3

> *I have loved you with an everlasting love;*
> *I have drawn you with unfailing kindness.*

Jen spoke of this incredible love that was available to anyone who wanted it. No conditions. No questions asked. No way to earn it. It's just simply there for us. You are loved by God.

It was at that conference that I opened my heart up to God and allowed Him to fill it with His love. And fill it, He did. God is not stingy with His love. He pours it out lavishly upon us. I finally realized that I am loved by God. Healing began for me that day. I finally realized that someone did love me, despite my flaws, and that I wasn't as alone as I thought I was. God knew every one of my mistakes and failures, He saw every detail about myself that I hated, He knew me intimately, inside and out, and He loved me.

The weekend continued with more powerful messages on God's love for us as well as an incredible opportunity to get to know other woman from our church and see that we all have flaws; even those people in the church who I looked up to had their own brokenness. As they opened up to me and shared their stories, I finally began to take off my own mask that I had been hiding behind for so long.

It was during that conference that I made the decision to give my life to God and find my identity in Him and what He says about me. I realized that God created me to be uniquely me, including my broken parts. I wasn't a mistake. I was created on purpose and for a purpose. My anxiety had told me so many lies about who I was, and I had formed my self-image based on those lies. But at that conference those lies were replaced by the identity that God gives me. The image I had created of myself was replaced by the image that God has of me and I began to see myself as God sees me- His beloved child.

So, what exactly does God say about who we are and what we mean to Him? The Bible tells us a lot about our identity in God. Let's take a look:

You are a Child of God- John 1:12
You are one with God in spirit- 1 Corinthians 6:17
You are no longer a slave to sin- Romans 6:6
You are made in God's image- Genesis 1:27
God knew you and planned for you before you were born- Jeremiah 1:5
Christ lives in you- Galatians 2:20
Jesus is your friend- John 15:15
God created you for good works- Ephesians 2:10
You have citizenship in heaven- Philippians 3:20
You were chosen by God- John 15:16
God delights in you- Zephaniah- 3:17
You are forgiven- 1 Peter 2:24
You are free- Galatians 5:1
You are a co-heir with Christ- Romans 8:17
You are an ambassador for Christ- 2 Corinthians 5:20
You are victorious- 1 John 5:4
You are never alone- Deuteronomy- 31:8
You are a masterpiece- Ephesians 2:10
You are wonderfully made- Psalm 139:14
You are blessed- 2 Corinthians 9:8
You are saved- Romans 10:9-10
Your future is secure- Jeremiah 29:11
You are a conqueror- Romans 8:37-39

and most importantly-

You are Loved- Jeremiah 31:3

These things are the truth of your identity in Jesus. When you are feeling unloved or unworthy, meditate on these verses and remember who you are.

It's like in the movie The Lion King. Simba goes through some horrible experiences that cause him to doubt and even deny who he is. He is afraid of what he has done and doesn't believe he could ever be loved or accepted again.

But eventually he is forced to choose to continue hiding or to face his fears and step into his destiny. In a vision, he hears the words "remember who you are."

When he finally does see the truth, and remembers who he really is, son of the great king, Mufasa, Simba is able to overcome all of the obstacles in his path.

Hopefully it doesn't take a whack on the head, like it did for Simba, to remember who you are. You, like Simba, are the child of a great King. But not just any king. You are a child of the King of kings and you are deeply loved for who you are, right now, right where you are.

After that conference, my anger, hatred for myself,

and my anxiety greatly diminished. I finally began to accept myself and accept the love God has for me. My confidence in myself grew. Not long after the conference, I felt called to lead a prayer at a Bible study I was attending. For someone who hates public speaking of any kind, and especially when it is something so personal, this was a big deal. God gave me the words to say and I had no fear at that moment. It was then that I understood what it meant to be filled with His Spirit.

In the next months and years, I would lead more prayers, lead a Vacation Bible School class, teach a Bible study, and become a girl's ministries leader. I would speak in front of the entire congregation on a few different occasions. I invited our women's group to the barn and shared my testimony of coming to faith with them. And, eventually I would travel to the other side of the globe with a group of strangers to share God's love with the people of Thailand.

The me, before that first conference, would never have believed that I would do any of those things. Anything is possible with God. He will take your broken life and broken heart, fill it with His incredible, unfailing love, and transform you into something new and beautiful.

There are still days when I struggle with fear and feeling unloved. New challenges continue to present themselves. Giving your life to God does not mean that every day will be sunshine and unicorns. It does, however, mean that God, through His love for you, will give you the strength you need to overcome.

No matter where you are in life right now or what you are going through, God loves you.

Remember who you are.

You are a child of the One True King.

You are Loved.

CHAPTER FIFTEEN:
PASSION

"Riding a horse is not a gentle hobby, to be picked up and laid down like a game of solitaire. It is a grand passion. It seizes a person whole and once it has done so, he/she will have to accept that his life will be radically changed." Ralph Waldo Emerson

"For once you have tasted flight you will walk the earth with your eyes turned skywards, for there you have been and there you will long to return."
Leonardo da Vinci

Working with horses is something that, if you let it, will take over your entire life. It changes your priorities, the way you spend your time and your money, and the way you think and act. You will begin to look at life differently through the eyes of a horse.

Becoming a horseman is a lifelong journey. There is always more to learn and to improve upon. Even the best horsemen in the world are constantly learning and growing. When you are passionate about something, you seek to better yourself and gain as much knowledge and experience as you can. With horses, this often means not just technical skills, but a deeper, stronger relationship with your horse.

As a riding instructor, it can be frustrating to see riders that have low ambitions for themselves and their horses. Now, of course not everyone desires to go to the Olympics or even be competitive, but there is more to riding horses than winning medals. There is the partnership and bond you develop with your horse. Once you experience this almost magical connection with your horse it becomes something you want to experience more and more.

When you only learn the basic mechanics of how to control a horse, you miss out on deeper understanding and fulfillment. Maybe you can lead a horse around, saddle him up and ride around at a basic walk, trot, or canter. But you don't understand how horses think and why they behave a certain way, and you don't try to improve your riding. You are happy with simply not falling off. Or maybe you have a horse that you don't do anything with at all. You may not even realize what you are missing out on.

The more we learn about our horses, like the way they think and behave, the stronger a relationship we can have with them. Think about the relationships you have with other people in your life. You can't develop a strong friendship with someone you know nothing about. First, you must spend time with them and learn about them. Only then, can the relationship be developed. Through continuously spending time and learning, the relationship is strengthened.

It is the same with our horses. We need to spend time with them and learn about them. This means developing our technical skills as well as learning about how our horses think, so we are better able to meet their needs and communicate with them.

This is the difference between a horse owner or rider and a true horseman. A horseman has a passion for horses and is always trying to improve themselves. He or she may not be the best rider out there, but technical skill is not what matters. True horsemen can be found anywhere like in the barn mucking out stalls, out enjoying a peaceful trail ride, in the field working on liberty skills, or in the competition ring showing off the bond and the skills they have developed. What unites them all is the passion that fuels them to never settle for where they are at, but instead to constantly grow and improve.

Many people will never develop that kind of a bond with their horse. It could be that they don't know it's possible. If that's you, I'm here to tell you that anyone can have this kind of a relationship with their horse. You don't have to be a guru or a horse whisperer. There is nothing magical about it. It simply takes time and effort.

Some people just don't want to put the work in. They put in the minimal effort and settle for the minimal results they achieve. They could have such a great partnership that would be so much more fulfilling, but they don't even try. They don't even realize what they are missing out on. I sometimes wonder if God feels this same way about us. He has such an incredible life planned out for us, but so often we are happy to settle for much less simply because we aren't willing to put the work in. I wonder what amazing things we miss out on and don't even realize it.

Christians often settle for the minimum in their spiritual lives as well. Maybe you go to church once a week and think that's enough, or you read your

Bible every once in a while, or pray when you need something, but that's really it. If you put minimal effort in, you will miss out on developing a stronger relationship with God, and you will miss out on the incredible life that God has for you.

God wants good things for us. He has plans for us that we can't even imagine. John 10:10 says "the thief comes only to steal and kill and destroy; I have come that they may have life and have it to the full." Following Jesus gives us a full and rewarding life. As we seek God and follow His plan for our lives, God will open doors for us to things we could never do without Him. So many of the most amazing experiences in my life have been a result of me seeking God and following His direction.

Jesus tells us, "I am the light of the world. Whoever follows me will never walk in darkness but will have the light of life." (John 8:12). Following Jesus brings light to our lives. A life seeking God brings joy.

It's not always easy. All relationships have struggles, including our relationship with God. All relationships require time and effort. We still go through difficult times, but we can take comfort knowing that God will always be there to help us. God is always rooting for us. He is our best friend and biggest fan. He will never leave us.

1 Timothy 6:12 tells us to "fight the good fight of the faith. Take hold of the eternal life to which you were called when you made your good confession in the presence of many witnesses."

God hopes that we will follow Him, not just half-heartedly, but to give Him our lives and follow Him passionately.

A relationship with God will take over and change your entire life. Following God is not something you only do on Sundays. Being a Christian is a way of living.

A relationship with God is the greatest thing that will ever happen in your life. It deserves to be developed and strengthened throughout your life. There will always be more to learn about God, and we can always deepen our relationship with Him. As we do, He brings fulfillment to our lives.

Psalm 16:11 says "you make known to me the path of life; in your presence there is fullness of joy; at your right hand are pleasures forevermore." (ESV)

Jesus also brings us freedom from our sins. The more we give our lives to Him, the more He is able to help us to overcome the things we struggle with.

Being a horseman is not just a job or a hobby, it's a lifestyle. It changes your entire perspective on life.

It's something that you think about all the time and put effort into.

In a similar way, being a Christian does not mean that you simply "do church" every Sunday. It means you give up your old way of living and commit yourself to a new and better lifestyle with Jesus at the center. It's not something you do every Sunday. It's something that takes over your entire life, every moment of every day.

Be passionate about life and about God! Do something worthwhile with your life. Too many people are spiritually apathetic. They are not passionate about God. They put minimal effort into their relationship with Him. These people have no idea the joy that they are missing out on. Once you experience it, it takes over your life and becomes something you constantly want more of.

When we constantly seek God and deepen our relationship with Him, He gives us a fuller life, free from sin, free from death, full of the Holy Spirit.

A life led by the Holy Spirit is an adventurous life. This means getting out there, leaving the safety of the walls of the church and getting out into the dirty, messy, and often scary world. Jesus calls us to follow Him and then to go out and make disciples. It's work. It takes time and dedication. It is done out of passion and a love for God and His people.

In my journey with horses, I've done many things that at one time I never would have believed possible. There was a time when even owning horses was a faraway dream. But I dedicated my life to pursuing my dreams and now we own four amazing Andalusians. With them I've performed movements of the highest levels of dressage. I've also be able to do some trick riding and vaulting, even standing on the back of a trotting horse. I've learned Roman Riding (standing on two horses at the same time). Through the liberty work, I've taken my partnership with my horses deeper than I ever could have imagined. It's been an amazing adventure that God has led me on.

Passionately pursuing my dreams has led to some incredible experiences with horses and also in my spiritual life.

My trip to Thailand was an incredible experience. But it was something I would have never considered doing on my own. It was only because I was seeking God's will and desiring a better relationship with Him that this opportunity was possible. God opened up all the right doors and steered me down the path to Thailand in a way that strengthened my faith and removed my fears.

It started in April 2015 at the Original Women's Conference at City First Church. This was the same conference that had led me to give my life to God a year earlier. The theme for the conference this year was Past the Wishing. One of the speakers encouraged us to make a list of things we would like to do but have held back out of fear or our busyness. I made my list and something caused me to write down that I'd like to go on a mission trip, though at the time I thought that would be something I would do way in the future so, I didn't think much more about it.

Several weeks after the Conference, City First sent out an email that they were taking applications for a short-term trip to Thailand. This brought me back to my list. The timing was a little too coincidental, but I did not think my first mission trip ever would be such a big one. Two weeks on the other side of the world and a $3000 price tag were a little too much for me. I ignored the email and didn't think about it again for another few weeks.

Then I found out that a friend was also considering going on the trip to Thailand. Funny how this trip kept coming up. I mentioned to her that I'd love to go on a trip someday but this one was too much for me. She encouraged me to go with her, but at the time I had said no. Now I was really starting to feel the tugging that happens when God wants you to do something. At that conference I had asked God to guide me on the path to a deeper relationship with

Him and that is exactly what He was doing.

The trip popped up a few more times over the next weeks, getting to the point where I really couldn't ignore it anymore. Eventually, I decided to ask God for one more confirmation. If He wanted me to go, I needed Him to provide the money to cover the application fee. It was not long after, He did just that. I had volunteered to help out with a funeral service at our church and I was given a thank you card. When I got home later that day and opened the card it contained inside of it the exact amount of money I needed for the application fee. God opened the door for me, and my path was set.

This trip took me out of my comfort zone in many different ways. I had never been on a mission trip before and the farthest out of the country I had been was Canada. The whole idea of taking a trip to the other side of the world with a group of people I didn't know very well seemed completely crazy and terrifying to me. This would also be the longest I'd been away from my wife since we were married and the longest time I'd been away from my business. I knew that in order to take this trip, I would have to lean heavily on God and put my trust in Him. I did, and God granted me an incredible experience.

While in Thailand, we worked with an organization called Zoe International. Zoe rescues children from human trafficking and gives them a safe place to stay. Kids at Zoe receive education, a family environment, and the unconditional love of Jesus.

The Zoe kids have been through things that most of us can't even imagine and yet they have come to know the love of Jesus. They are so filled with joy and love for others. These kids have such strong faith. They don't question things or over complicate them. These kids have seen utter darkness. However, they have also seen the Light. They know how much they have to be thankful for, so they cannot wait to throw themselves at the feet of Jesus and to give Him their whole lives. At Zoe, everyone was so focused on God in everything they did. It was easy to feel God's presence, seeing the work that He was doing and to feel especially close to Him.

Prayer is a priority for everyone at Zoe, both the leaders and the children. They are not timid but pray and worship loudly and boldly. They are not shy about praying for each other. They are constantly seeking out God and His will for them.

During one of our outreaches, we went out into a small village up in the mountains. We went house to house to invite people to our event that evening, to pray for them, and if they were willing to share the Gospel. The Zoe ministry students took the lead as none of these villagers spoke English. We were there to support the ministry students and to be in constant prayer for both the students and the villagers.

Maybe you've heard of being able to see Jesus in people. As we were sitting there on the wooden floors of the huts, I could literally see Jesus in the students as they shared the Gospel with the villagers. I've never seen anyone so on fire for Jesus and so passionate about sharing His love. I couldn't understand the words they were saying but I could feel the power of God working through them.

We were able to pray for several people including a lady who was 9 months pregnant, an elderly woman who had been baptized but didn't understand what that meant, and another elderly woman who had limited mobility because of pain in her legs. After we prayed for her, she was able to stand and walk without pain. Another team prayed for a young man who could not speak. After they prayed, he spoke the words "God bless you."

After my trip, people kept telling me how brave I was to go and how they could never do what I did. I think people think that missionary work is for "super Christians", that only special people can do that kind of work. But I am just a normal person. I'm not brave. I am a very fearful person. In fact, fear has kept me from doing many things that I've wanted to and has held me back from doing things God has asked me to do. I've failed God far more times than I've obeyed Him. This trip was a completely crazy idea to me and there was no way I could have done it on my own. God doesn't need you to be able to handle everything on your own; He often takes you out of your comfort zone so you will learn to trust Him and depend on Him. He walked with me through every single step of the process and my faith in Him is so much stronger as a result, all because I was willing to keep seeking Him.

My faith is stronger after taking this step of faith and seeing how God was able to work through every step of it. I'm starting to see that God is faithful. When He calls us to do something, we just need to trust Him.

No one is more committed to the call on your life than He who calls you. When God calls you to do something, He is committed to helping you through it.

My theme song for this trip was the song Oceans. God called me out of my comfort zone and out onto the waves of the ocean, just like He called Peter out of the boat. And through it all He remained faithful. He took my hand and walked every step with me as we left my comfort zone behind and stepped into His incredible plan for me. Ever since making a commitment to follow Christ, He has continually called me farther and farther out onto the waves. I've done things that I never thought I could. It's been quite an adventure.

Don't settle for where you are. Follow God passionately, let Him guide your life, and get ready for experiences you've never even dreamed of. He loves you more than you will ever know, and He has most wonderful things planned for you. Whether you just started following God or you've been following Him for years, He has more for you. Seeking God is a lifelong journey. Give Him your life, give Him your trust, and enjoy the ride!

"Adventure is out there."

-Walt Disney

CONCLUSION

Thank you for sharing this journey with me. God has given us hooved angels to show us the way to Him. They will help us and guide us faithfully until the day when heaven opens up and Jesus returns to Earth, riding upon one of these noble steeds.

I saw heaven standing open and there before me was a white horse, whose rider is called Faithful and True. With justice he judges and wages war. His eyes are like blazing fire, and on his head are many crowns. He has a name written on him that no one knows but He himself. He is dressed in a robe dipped in blood, and his name is the Word of God. The armies of heaven were following him, riding on white horses and dressed in fine linen, white and clean. Coming out of his mouth is a sharp sword with which to strike down the nations. "He will rule them with an iron scepter." He treads the winepress of the fury of the wrath of God Almighty. On His robe and on His thigh, He has this name written:

KING OF KINGS AND LORD OF LORDS

Revelation 19:11-16

FURTHER STUDY

Verse to Remember-

The Lord will fight for you; you need only to be still. Exodus 14:14

When was the last time you spent time with your horse just enjoying each other's presence?

How can you practice "being still" with your horse?

In what ways or areas of your life do you struggle to let things go and trust God?

How can you incorporate "being still" into your life? This will be different for everyone. It may be prayer or meditation, worship, or reading your Bible. Be sure this doesn't become just another task. It should be a time to rest and recover. Not something to check off your list.

Recall a time when you felt close to God. What was it like?

Chapter Two: Overcoming Fear

Verse to Remember-

For God has not given us a spirit of fear, but of power, and of love, and of a sound mind. 1 Timothy 1:7 (KJV)

Have you worked with a fearful horse before? How have you been able to help them overcome their fears?

Has there been a time when God has helped you through something you were afraid of?

Is there a fear in your life right now that you are struggling with?

How can you improve your "practice time" with the Armor of God?

Take another look at the armor of God described in Ephesians. Now take a look at your own personal armor. Where is it the strongest? Where are the weaknesses? What can you do to strengthen your armor?

Chapter Three: Following God

Verse to Remember-

Trust in the Lord with all your heart and lean not on your own understanding; in all your ways acknowledge him and he will make straight your path. Proverbs 3:5-6

In what ways have you asked your horse to trust you? How did he/she respond?

In what ways can you be a good leader and guide for your horse?

Are there any events in the past you can recall that seemed scary or confusing at the time but had a good outcome?

In what situations right now is God asking you to trust Him?

Chapter Four: Enjoy the Process

Verse to Remember-

Let us not become weary in doing good, for at the proper time we will reap a harvest if we do not give up. Galatians 6:9

What is something you've accomplished with your horse that you never thought you would be able to?

What is something you've accomplished in your spiritual life that you never thought you would be able to?

Is there something that you feel discouraged about right now? How can you ask God to help you be patient with His timing and keep moving forward?

Are the people around you encouraging you in your journey? Are there changes you need to make so you are surrounded by people who will build you up rather than tear you down?

Chapter Five: Overcoming Failure

Verse to Remember-

I can do all this through him who gives me strength. Philippians 4:13

What struggles or failures have you been able to overcome with your horse?

Describe a time when you thought you had failed but God was able to turn it around for good.

How has God helped you to overcome your failures and difficulties?

Is there anything you are struggling with right now? Ask God for help to trust Him and His plan for you.

Chapter Six: Free Will

Verse to Remember-

For God so loved the world that he gave his one and

only Son, that whoever believes in Him shall not perish but have eternal life. John 3:16

How have you seen people use force in horse training? What about kindness? Have you noticed a difference in the reactions of the horses based on how they are treated?

What are some of the ways God has shown His love to you?

What are some ways you can share God's love with others? Don't just think vaguely. Try to come up with some real actions you can be intentional about doing this week or this month.

Chapter Seven: Surrender

Verse to Remember-

I have been crucified with Christ and I no longer live, but Christ lives in me. The life I now live in the body, I live by faith in the Son of God, who loved me and gave himself for me. Galatians 2:20

What paths has God taken you on that you haven't expected?

How can you help your horse to trust and surrender to you?

Considering the similarity of surrendering to God

and your horse surrendering to you, does that change how you view your horse and the relationship you have with your horse?

Do you trust God enough to do things that don't make sense remembering that God's understanding far exceeds our own?

How have you experienced God pour his living water into you?

How has God's living water flowed out of you?

Chapter Eight: Mirroring

Verse to Remember-

Therefore be imitators of God, as beloved children. And walk in love, as Christ loved us and gave himself up for us, a fragrant offering and sacrifice to God. Ephesians 5:2 (ESV)

Have you ever noticed your horse reflect your emotions, feelings, energy level, or personality? In what ways?

What are some ways you can be an encouragement to your horse? What about to those around you?

How can you imitate the love that God has for all of His people?

Verse to remember-

Love the Lord your God with all your heart and with all your soul and with all your strength and with all your mind. Luke 10:27

Describe any experiences you have had working with a distracted horse. What about a focused horse? What are some of the differences you noticed between the two?

How does your horse respond when you lose focus?

Describe a time when you lost focus on God? What happened? How were you able to get your focus back on God?

Describe a time when you've been able to use the Word to help you overcome temptation. What are some of the verses that have helped you the most?

Chapter Ten: Sensitivity

Verse to Remember-

And do not bring sorrow to God's Holy Spirit by the way you live. Remember, he has identified you as his own, guaranteeing that you will be saved on the day of redemption. Ephesians 4:30 (NLT)

How can you become more sensitive to your horse's needs?

Have you ridden a horse that is sensitive to the rider's cues? What about a horse that is dull? Explain how each felt.

How can you help encourage your horse to stay sensitive or to learn to become sensitive?

How can you stay sensitive to God's heart and His will for your life?

Share an experience where you felt in tune with God. Share an experience when you felt distanced from God. How did you feel during each of these times?

Chapter Eleven: Humility

Verse to Remember-

Have this mind among yourselves, which is yours in Christ Jesus, who, though he was in the form of God, did not count equality with God a thing to be grasped, but emptied himself, by taking the form of a servant, being born in the likeness of men. And being found in human form, he humbled himself by becoming obedient to the point of death, even death on a cross. Philippians 2:5-8

Share an example of a time when you learned humility from working with horses.

What are some ways you can serve others around you?

In what areas of your life do you struggle with pride? Take those things to God in prayer and ask Him to help you let go of your need for pride.

Chapter Twelve: Forgiveness

Verse to Remember-

But God demonstrates His own love for us in this: While we were still sinners, Christ died for us. Romans 5:8

Was there a time when you experienced forgiveness from your horse?

Describe an experience when you forgave someone, or someone forgave you. Were you able to let go of hurt feelings?

Describe a time that God offered His forgiveness to you.

Is there anyone who you need to forgive? Ask God for the strength and then make the choice to forgive and continue forgiving.

Chapter Thirteen: Authenticity

Verse to remember-

Am I now trying to win the approval of human beings, or of God? Or am I trying to please people? If I were still trying to please people, I would not be a servant of Christ. Galatians 1:10

Are there areas of your life or parts of who you are that you are hiding?

Learning to become more authentic is a process. Start small. Is there one person that you can open up to and be more authentic with?

How can you help others around you feel comfortable being their authentic selves?

Chapter Fourteen: Unconditional Love

Verse to Remember-

I have loved you with an everlasting love; I have drawn you with unfailing kindness. Jeremiah 31:3

What are some ways you have experienced unconditional love with horses?

Describe your bond with your horse.

Is there a time when you have been transformed by God's love? Maybe He gave you strength or helped you overcome something? Or maybe He changed your outlook on a situation? Maybe He was there for you when no one else was?

Have you opened your heart to God's love and invited Him into your life? If so, what was that experience like? If not, you can do so right now. Just ask God to fill you with His love. He is so eager to do so; He is just waiting for you to ask.

Chapter Fifteen: Passion

Verse to Remember-

The thief comes only to steal and kill and destroy; I have come that they may have life, and have it to the full. John 10:10

What are some ways you can improve your horsemanship?

Learning new things helps strengthen a relationship. What is something you are working on with your horse or learning about your horse right now?

What are some ways you can learn more about God or deepen your relationship with Him?

What are some adventures God has taken you on?

What are some next steps you can take in your

adventure with God? Maybe you are just starting out and the next step is joining a church or a Bible Study. Maybe learning more about God by studying His word is your next step. Maybe it's adopting a child, getting involved with a charity, or going on a missions trip, or maybe it's going across the street to meet your neighbors and invite them to church.

God is calling you to step out of your comfort zone and join Him on the waves. Leave behind the false security of the boat and get ready for a great adventure.

REFERENCES

1. Barbier, Dominque. (2011). *Mediation for Two* . Trafalger Square Books.

2. Henry, Matthew. (1996, March 1). *Commentary on Exodus 14.* Retrieved from Blue Letter Bible: https://www.blueletterbible.org/Comm/mhc/Exd/Exd_014.cfm

3. Guzik, David. (2017, February 21). *A Study Guide for Philippians 4.* Retrieved from Blue Letter Bible: https://www.blueletterbible.org/Comm/guzik_david/StudyGuide2017-Phl/Phl-4.cfm

4. Spurgeon, Charles. (2017). *Spurgeon's Sermons Volume 15: 1869.* Devoted Publishing.

5. Rolfe, Jenny. (2005). *Ride from the Heart.* J.A. Allen.

6. Lewis, C.S. (2008). *The Magician's Nephew.* Harper Collins, Reprint Edition.

7. Lewis, C.S. (2015). *Mere Christianity.* HarperOne.

8. Buttigieg, Pete. (2019, May 11). (Human Rights Dinner)

9. Lucado, Max. (2000). *Grace for the Moment.* J Countryman.

10. Henry, Matthew. (1996, March 1). *Commentary on Ephesians 4.* Retrieved from Blue Letter Bible: https://www.blueletterbible.org/Comm/mhc/Eph/Eph_004.cfm

11. Kohanov, Linda. (2015, March 19). *The Hidden Wisdom of Feeling.* Retrieved from Epona Quest: https://eponaquest.com/hidden-wisdom-of-feeling-emotional-fitness-for-equestrians/

ABOUT THE AUTHOR

Bethany's love of horses began at an early age. She has dedicated her life to learning the art of horsemanship. She has studied classical dressage, liberty work, trick training, work-in-hand, and long-reining and is the founder of Tuskey Dressage, offering lessons and training for riders looking to improve their horsemanship. Through relationships built on trust and respect, Bethany is able to train horses to the highest levels of dressage or at complete freedom in liberty work without any use of force. Bethany also enjoys performing with her Andalusians at various shows and exhibitions. It is her desire to share her unique training style and help people to take their relationships both with their horse, and with God, to a deeper level.

Bethany lives in Wisconsin with her wife, Nicole, and their son Zeke, along with their four horses and other pets.

Bethany would love to hear your stories of your journey with horses and with God. You may email her anytime at tuskeydressage@gmail.com

For more information about Tuskey Dressage visit tuskeydressage.com